HEMINGWAY'S KEY WEST

SECOND EDITION

HEMINGWAY'S KEY WEST

SECOND EDITION

Stuart B. McIver

Pineapple Press, Inc.
Sarasota, Florida

Inquiries should be addressed to:
Pineapple Press, Inc.
P.O. Box 3889
Sarasota, Florida 34230

www.pineapplepress.com

Library of Congress Cataloging-in-Publication Data

McIver, Stuart B.
Hemingway's Key West / Stuart B. McIver.—2nd ed.
cm.
Includes bibliographical references and index.
ISBN 1-56164-241-X (pbk. : alk. paper)
1. Hemingway, Ernest, 1899–1961—Homes and haunts—Florida—Key West. 2. Hemingway, Ernest, 1899–1961—Homes and haunts—Bahamas—Bimini Islands. 3. Hemingway, Ernest, 1899–1961—Homes and haunts—Cuba. 4. Bimini Islands (Bahamas)—Social life and customs. 5. Americans—Bahamas—Bimini Islands—Biography. 6. Authors, American—20th century—Biography. 7. Key West (Fla.)—Social life and customs. 8. Cuba—Social life and customs. 9. Americans—Cuba—Biography. I. Title.

PS3515.E37 Z74118 2001
813'.52—dc21
[B]

2001023495

Second Edition
10 9 8 7 6 5 4 3 2 1

Design by Robert Fleury
Printed in the United States of America

TABLE OF CONTENTS

ACKNOWLEDGMENTS

Many people deserve thanks for their insight, information, and encouragement during the many years this project took. Their help ranged from smoothing over a rough spot to contributing so much that this book couldn't have been completed without them. Here they are: Danilo Arrate, John Boisonault, Betty and Toby Bruce, Belkys Cedeno, Ruth Chados, Sir Michael Checkley, Jane Day, Ossie Davis, Gregorio Fuentes, Tom Hambright, Jeff Storm Harkavy, Rosemary Jones, John Klausing, Linda Larson, Hilary Hemingway, Lorian Hemingway, Mina Hemingway, Wright and Joan Langley, Michael Leech, Evadne Stewart Masters, Gail Morchower, Joan Morris, Jim Plath, Stephen Plotkin, Sylvia Robards, Gladys Ferrero Rodriguez, Carmen Roque, Carol and Edmund Sadowski, Bickford Sylvester, Jean Trebbi, Michael Whalton, Arthur Valladares, Jeff "Gator" Wilson, and Molly Wylly.

HEMINGWAY'S KEY WEST

SECOND EDITION

❖

CHAPTER I

❖ ❖ ❖ ❖ ❖ ❖ ❖ ❖ ❖ ❖ ❖ ❖

ISLANDS IN THE STREAM

ERNEST MILLER HEMINGWAY WAS BORN ON July 21, 1899, in Oak Park, Illinois, a suburb of the Windy City, as the cold, northern metropolis of Chicago was called without affection on those days when icy winds swept in from Lake Michigan. After World War I, he lived in Paris, where the rich intellectual and artistic climate was warm and inviting to a young writer. But the winters were cold and wet. In the spring of 1928, he sought out for the first time the heat of the islands in the stream—the Gulf Stream.

His goal that April was Florida's southernmost island, Key West. The ship bearing Ernest and his second wife, Pauline Pfeiffer, stopped briefly in Cuba, which lay on the south side of the stream. Key West lay roughly ninety miles away on the north side of the Gulf Stream.

The warm currents of the Gulf of Mexico accelerate as they flow through the narrows between Mexico's Yucatan Peninsula and the Florida Keys. The stream then turns east through the Florida Straits before veering north past the Bahama Islands and the fishing paradise called Bimini. Continuing their northern flow, the soothing waters of the stream eventually bring warmth to Bermuda, the British Isles, and such icy islands as Iceland and Greenland.

1

However, the northern islands are not the ones that enthralled Hemingway.

Key West, Bimini, Cuba—these are the three islands in the stream that claimed the allegiance of Hemingway for the final three decades of his life. Of the three, only Cuba lies south of the Tropic of Cancer, thus qualifying it as a tropical island. But both Key West and Bimini are generally regarded as tropical isles, partly because of their heat, their palm trees, and the beauty of the waters surrounding them. And partly because, in a phrase not known in Hemingway's day, they were "laid-back." These were easygoing, unconventional locales where a man could soothe a thirst, stroll around barefooted all year long, and go about his business free from the pressures of too much civilization.

Key West was and is a small town, as is Alice Town, the largest town on Bimini. Havana by contrast is a big, sprawling city, the largest in the Caribbean, known from early Colonial times as the Pearl of the Antilles. For his Cuban home, Hemingway chose to live not in the bustling, energetic capital but in San Francisco de Paula, a small town west of Havana.

In addition to year-round hot weather, all three islands had in common one major asset—fishing. As a boy, Ernest turned to the streams of northern Michigan. Casting for freshwater fish tested his sporting skills. Catching the giant sea creatures of the Gulf Stream required much more than skill. It demanded strategy, strength, endurance, and knowledge of the behavior of the huge fish and the other ocean predators that might also be seeking the same game as the deep-sea angler. Fishing in the stream was for Hemingway a challenge, and he was a man who pursued challenge.

His biggest challenge, of course, was to reach for new heights in literature. His years on the islands were productive, but only two of his novels were about the sea. In one, *The Old Man and the Sea*, he achieved a masterpiece. As for the other, *Islands in the Stream*, we will never know how great it might have been. Published after his death,

2

it lacked the final meticulous revision he brought to his best work. The reader has to settle for many wonderful passages, settings, and characters.

All three of his islands have changed since his death some four decades ago. But one thing has proved constant. The presence of Ernest Hemingway remains alive and well in Key West, Bimini, and Cuba, Hemingway's islands in the stream.

❖

CHAPTER II

❖ ❖ ❖ ❖ ❖ ❖ ❖ ❖ ❖ ❖ ❖

BONE KEY

JUST THE PLACE for "Ole Hem . . . to dry out his bones." That was the recommendation John Dos Passos made to fellow novelist Ernest Hemingway. And, in fact, Hemingway's bones could use a good drying out. He had spent another cold, wet winter in his apartment on Paris's Left Bank.

Key West was a perfect choice for a man with cold bones. The island had once been called *Cayo Hueso,* Spanish for Bone Key. It was supposedly the site of an ancient Indian massacre that had left its sands covered with sun-bleached skeletons. The bones had long ago been cleared out but part of the name stuck. Cayo Hueso was Anglicized into Key West.

The southernmost city in the United States, Key West was well placed to pour on all the heat the author could stand. It missed being a tropical island by less than a hundred miles, a whim of geography that did little to compromise the key's Caribbean spirit: laid-back, relaxed, tolerant.

In every sense, Key West, some seven thousand miles to the southwest of Paris, was a far cry from the French metropolis. By the 1920s, the cosmopolitan French metropolis had become the artistic and intellectual capital of the world—home of Picasso, Chagall, Dali,

Cubism, Art Deco, Dada, the Ballets Russes, Nijinksy, Pavlova, *le jazz hot*, Coco Chanel, James Joyce, Gertrude Stein, and, not incidentally, Ernest Hemingway.

Key West was, by contrast, a mess. By 1928 its population had shrunk from twenty-six thousand to ten thousand. Jobs were moving away as fast as a hooked tarpon's run. A blight had wiped out the sponge industry. The Cuban cigar industry moved away to Tampa, leaving little but the rhythms of Spanish speech and the aroma of black bean soup. With onions. Conchs eked out a living by fishing commercially or by smuggling booze from Havana. No wonder Ernest dubbed the town "the St. Tropez of the Poor."

Key West had no literary, no artistic, no intellectual life. Hemingway would change that. The island the expatriate writer had planned to visit as a vacation hideaway would become the only American city where he could live and work as an adult. Just the place for "Ole Hem . . . to dry out his bones."

❖ ❖ ❖

Ernest Hemingway first saw Key West in April 1928. That spring he and his second wife, Pauline Pfeiffer Hemingway, five months pregnant, sailed from Marseilles to Havana. From there they boarded a Peninsular & Occidental steamship bound for the island, just ninety miles away. As the ship crossed the swift, dark Gulf Stream and maneuvered through the Florida Reef, he gazed across clear aqua waters and saw ahead a flat, grayish mass broken only by the town's skyscraper, the seven-story Colonial Hotel, rising like a thick, Key West cigar from a clump of wooden, mostly unpainted buildings. Only as the ship steamed closer could he begin to make out the island's colors—the brilliant tropical foliage, bougainvillea, hibiscus, oleander—interspersed with green palm fronds.

The heat bothered the Hemingways. Ernest was not dressed for Key West. He was wearing a necktie, hardly part of the town's dress code. Pregnancy made the weather harder for Pauline to take. She wanted her baby born in the United States, but clearly not in a hot, humid, run-down backwater like Key West. The couple planned to stay in Key West only about six weeks and then drive to Piggott, Arkansas, the ancestral home of the Pfeiffers.

Shortly before noon they cleared customs, and Ernest began looking for the Model A Ford roadster Pauline's wealthy Uncle Gus had bought for them. Unfortunately, the car had not yet arrived from

Florida Photographic Archives

Ernest Hemingway at the typewriter. He actually preferred to write in longhand.

Miami. Ernest telephoned the Trevor and Morris Company, the local Ford dealership. Apologetic that the car was late, the dealers insisted that the couple take up residence at one of the Trevor and Morris Apartments, upstairs over the garage. A sweat-drenched, irritated Hemingway agreed. He called a taxi to take them and their luggage the four blocks from the P&O docks to their new quarters at 314 Simonton Street.

Without the delay, Hemingway's stay in Key West might have been a short one. Fortunately he stayed long enough to realize that the island was right for him. Once he got the necktie off, he enjoyed the bone-warming heat. He promptly went to work on a half-finished manuscript that would become *A Farewell to Arms*. In Paris he had lived and worked in an apartment above a sawmill. Now he found himself trying to complete his novel above a small-town garage. It was, he remarked, a kind of irony he could "damn well do without."

Alvin Morland, a Florida travel writer, visited the island as a boy during the early Hemingway years. A story he wrote later gave some of the flavor of the times: "We arrived in Key West during the siesta hour when most businesses were closed, but the aroma of strong Cuban coffee permeated the downtown area. The unpainted homes, weathered gray, had balconies. Their sloping roofs were designed to funnel rain water into pipes leading to cisterns, the only source of fresh water in the city. There seemed to be ice cream parlors in every block of the commercial section, and we wasted no time in trying such exotic flavors as coconut, sugar apple and sapodilla. Later we sampled *marquitas*—fried green plantains sliced as thin as potato chips."

Soon after he settled in, Hemingway received a letter forwarded from Paris. The letter informed him that his parents, Dr. Clarence Hemingway, a physician, and his wife, Grace, were in Florida. His father, whose home was in Oak Park, Illinois, was inspecting land he owned in St. Petersburg. Actually Ernest's parents were a good bit closer. The writer was fishing from the Trumbo pier when he heard a familiar bobwhite whistle. It was a family signal. He looked up and saw his father waving to him from a P&O steamship.

Ernest was saddened to observe his father's deteriorating health. He was, however, glad that his parents got along quite well with Pauline. The four of them had dinner downtown, probably at Delmonico's at 218 Duval Street. For fifty cents the restaurant featured a representative Cuban/Key West dinner of arroz con pollo, green turtle steak, fish, and Spanish garbanzos. After a tour of the island guided by Ernest, the Hemingways boarded the 5:40 P.M. train for Miami.

A week after Ernest and Pauline landed at Key West, Uncle Gus's yellow roadster was delivered. Soon Hemingway was driving up the highway some twenty miles to the No Name Key ferryboat docks and fishing from the landing there.

One day George "Georgie" Brooks, prosecuting attorney for Monroe County, was waiting for the ferryboat from Lower Matecumbe Key. He noticed a new face, a big, rugged fisherman wearing canvas shorts, a fish-stained pullover shirt, a cap, and dirty tennis shoes. No doubt about it—the man looked suspicious. Scars above his right knee—from an Austrian .420 shell wound in World War I—and a particularly nasty purple scar above his right eye. Could the man with the rod and reel be a lawbreaker on the run? Or another bootlegger?

Striking up a conversation with him, Brooks soon put his suspicions to rest. The man was writing a book, he said, and resting up after a "bloody awful" winter in Paris. Hemingway probably dodged around any questions about the purple scar, the result of an embarrassingly bizarre accident in France. In the wee hours of a cold March morning he had gone to the bathroom in his apartment. He had sleepily reached up for the chain to flush the toilet. Instead he grasped the cord to the skylight. The glass came crashing down on his head. Nine stitches in an emergency room at 3 A.M. had closed the nasty wound.

Hemingway asked Brooks if he knew anyone with a boat who would be willing to share fishing expenses. The attorney told him to go to the Thompson Hardware Store on Caroline Street and introduce himself to Charles Thompson.

"He likes to fish as well as any man I know," said Brooks. "He'll take you out. Just tell him I sent you by."

The lawyer would become one of Hemingway's closest friends, but not as close as the man he sent him to see. Ernest picked up his rod and reel and the hog snappers he had caught and drove back to Key West.

Clad in khakis, Charles, a member of the island's most affluent family, was standing behind a counter when Hemingway walked in. Their handshake initiated one of the most enduring friendships of the author's life. They made arrangements to go out fishing the next evening. After he closed the store, Charles walked to his home at 1029 Fleming Street. That night he told his wife, Lorine, about the man he had met.

"Georgie Brooks sent him by. Says his name's Hemingway. Said George told him I liked to fish and might take him out. Says he's written a couple of books."

A couple of books? By April 1928, the twenty-nine-year-old Hemingway already had six published books to his credit, most notably *Men Without Women*, a volume of short stories, and the internationally acclaimed novel, *The Sun Also Rises*. He was a celebrity in Paris and in much of the United States. But in Key West he was an unknown. And he liked it that way.

❖

CHAPTER III

❖ ❖ ❖ ❖ ❖ ❖ ❖ ❖ ❖ ❖ ❖

HEMINGWAY'S MOB

THE DAY AFTER HEMINGWAY MET THOMPSON, the two of them boarded Charles's eighteen-foot powerboat and followed the channel through Key West Bight to the Gulf of Mexico. An evening of fishing brought them several sizable tarpon, a fighting game fish known as the Silver King. The magic of Key West was beginning to seduce Ernest. Free of distractions, he could concentrate on *A Farewell to Arms* during the mornings, then relax in the afternoons or evenings with a rod and reel.

Soon Thompson invited the Hemingways over to dinner at their home, only a few blocks away from the Trevor and Morris Apartments. Lorine entertained them in true Key West style. She had Phoebe, her black Bahamian cook, prepare a conch dinner for the visitors, who had only recently dined in the brasseries of Paris. Phoebe cooked black beans and yellow rice and a Keys' delicacy, green turtle steak. One of the many businesses of the affluent Thompson family was a cannery that processed turtle meat for steaks and soup. To round out the meal, Phoebe served them a raw conch-meat salad and Cuban bread. Ernest brought a European touch to the occasion with several bottles of good red Chianti wine.

Hemingway lavishly praised the island cooking. Phoebe was delighted. "That mon Hemnway one fine eater," she said.

10

Ernest also offered impressive proof that he was indeed an author. He gave Charles a copy of *The Sun Also Rises*, inscribed "To Charles Thompson from his friend Ernest Hemingway, Key West 1928," and a copy of *Men Without Women*, with an even more personal message, "To Charles Thompson with all best wishes—and many tarpon—from his friend Ernest Hemingway, Key West, 1928."

It was a good evening for all concerned. Ernest and Charles had a few Scotches after dinner, then walked along tree-shaded Fleming Street, talking about hunting and fishing. Pregnant Pauline, increasingly uncomfortable in the stuffy apartment, relaxed with Lorine on the Thompson's breezy front porch. As they talked, a bond began to form between them that paralleled the closeness their husbands were building. The two men and the two women would remain friends the rest of their lives.

A native of Georgia, Lorine graduated from Agnes Scott College in Decatur, near Atlanta, in 1919. Two years later, she came to Key West to teach social science and soon became head of the Social Science Department at Key West High School. She married Charles on September 6, 1923. Pauline, an heiress, had graduated from the University of Missouri. In France she had been a fashion writer for the Paris edition of *Vogue* magazine. The two women found they had much in common. Both had been born in rural communities in the South, both had been well educated, and both had moved out into a bigger world.

Pauline's father, Paul Pfeiffer, president of the Piggott Custom Gin Company, came to Key West to see his new son-in-law. Pauline and Ernest installed him in the Key West Colonial Hotel, the town's seven-story skyscraper. Pauline, anxious to get away from the heat, wanted the three of them to drive to Piggott. Ernest protested. He finally agreed to let her leave early by train with a promise that he and her father would follow shortly.

Hemingway liked to surround himself with a circle of cronies, a "Mob." He sent out letters inviting a number of old friends to join him in the "St. Tropez of the Poor." He wrote to two artist friends, Henry Strater and Waldo Peirce; Bill Smith, a boyhood friend from Horton Bay, Michigan; and John Dos Passos.

While awaiting their arrival, he added to his Mob a number of locals whose company he enjoyed. With the exception of Charles, most of them were saddled with colorful nicknames. Joe Russell, a Conch who owned two basic generators of income—a charter boat and a speakeasy—was "Josie" or "Sloppy Joe," a name he gave to a legal bar he opened after Prohibition was repealed. Four other charter boat fishermen were Mobsters: Hamilton Adams ("Sack of Ham" or "Sacker"); Captain Eddie Saunders ("Bra") and his half-brother, Captain Burge Saunders; and Jakie Key. A local newspaperman, Earl Adams, became "Jewfish." Adams, who became a close friend, was Keys bureau chief for the *Miami Herald.* During his newspaper days he also worked for the *Key West Citizen,* the *Key West Morning Journal,* and the *Baltimore International News.* J. B. Sullivan, an Irishman who owned a machine shop, was "Sully." Ernest had his share of nicknames. He was called the "Old Master," and after being observed with a towel wrapped around his head he was also classified as the "Mahatma." Later in Key West he would assume the father-image name he liked best, "Papa."

By the last week in May, all the out-of-town talent had arrived: Dos Passos ("Dos"), Henry Strater ("Mike"), Waldo Peirce ("Don Pico"), and Bill Smith ("Old Bill.") Bypassing the island's luxury hotel, the Casa Marina, with rooms "from $7," Ernest booked them into the one-hundred-room Overseas Hotel, a three-story wood hostelry at 917 Fleming Street. Room rates: a dollar a day. Charles pronounced them "as grand a group of men as ever came together."

Thompson connections gave them access to the clear blue-green waters at the Navy Yard. There the men swam together and cheered and jeered at Hemingway's specialty dive, a combination of belly buster and swan dive. They called it the "Hemingswan."

For breakfast they liked the bare-bones Electric Kitchen, a one-story wooden building at 830 Fleming Street. The owner and cook was Mrs. Rhoda Baker, better known as "Rutabaga." A "club break-fast" at the Electric Kitchen cost 20 to 45 cents; lunch and dinner, 30 to 50 cents. When they went together as a group for dinner, they usually picked Delmonico's or Ramon's, both on Duval Street. Some of their dinners were enjoyed at the Thompsons' home, where they feasted on the cooking of Phoebe.

After one of Phoebe's dinners, they often strolled east on Fleming Street to Valladares Book Store, where they browsed through books and magazines. Leonte Valladares, a thirty-year-old Cuban, had agreed to stock Hemingway's hardback books. He charged a dollar extra for autographed copies of *The Sun Also Rises* and *Men Without Women*. Through Valladares, Hemingway subscribed to the New York papers—the *Times,* the *Herald-Tribune,* the *World-Telegram,* the *Mirror,* and the *Daily News.* The papers were delivered by the proprietor's young son, Arthur. He recalled his first meeting with Hemingway:

Florida Photographic Archives

Duval Street in the 1930s when Hemingway's Mob ranged up and down the streets of Key West.

13

"He came into my father's store, wearing moccasins and a pair of shorts held up with a rope. 'This man is poor; he doesn't have a belt,' I said to my father in Spanish. What I didn't know was that Hemingway understood Spanish. He picked me up and sat me down in his lap and told me in Spanish an Indian legend about how moccasins were made."

A rowdy bunch, the Mob liked to carouse in the evenings. One of their favorite places was Raul's Club on East Roosevelt Boulevard, commanding a view of the Atlantic. A live orchestra played and couples danced on "the finest dance floor in the city." A bizarre feature was a tank of groupers trained by Raul Vasquez himself to perform in their tank as he fed them by hand. In Old Town they visited Pena's Garden of Roses, a beer garden nestled among rose bushes. Another popular spot was the Tropical Club on the corner of Front and Fitzpatrick Streets. Its sign called it the place "where good fellows get together." At 1111 Duval Street, they visited the Cuban Cafe, which offered "foreign and domestic beer—anything you want."

To cap off the first assembling of the Mob, Ernest planned a weekend fishing trip to the Dry Tortugas. He hired Captain Bra Saunders and his charter boat, along with Bra's brother, Burge, as mate. On a Friday afternoon in the third week in May they set out for the islands west of Key West—Ernest, Dos, Don Pico, Mike, and the poet Archibald MacLeish, an old friend from Paris who had joined them in Key West. Charles trailed Captain Bra's charter boat in his eighteen-footer. Burge rode with him.

Just before dusk they anchored in the Marquesas Islands. They swam in the clear waters near their boat and caught fish for dinner, unaware that underneath the Gulf's sandy bottom lay the three-hundred-million-dollar treasure of the *Nuestra Senora de Atocha*, a Spanish galleon wrecked on the reef in 1622. Next morning at dawn, they arose for a breakfast of thick Cuban coffee, Cuban bread, avocados, and smoked fish.

Both boats went out in quest of the Silver King, the giant tarpon for which the Marquesas were famous. The prize went to the rugged, bearded Waldo Peirce, who battled a 183½ pound tarpon for two hours before pulling it to shore.

Early the next morning, a low-pressure ridge convinced Charles, a man who knew the vagaries of Keys weather, that he had better head his eighteen-footer back to safe harbor closer to Key West. Captain Bra's charter boat continued its westward cruise toward the Dry Tortugas. Just before dark, Captain Bra tied up at the docks at historic Fort Jefferson. Built before the Civil War as a defense outpost and a coaling station, Fort Jefferson later became famous as the prison that housed Dr. Samuel Mudd, the Maryland doctor who set the broken leg of John Wilkes Booth after the assassination of President Abraham Lincoln. Don Pico's fishing skills deserted him in the Tortugas. He hooked, then lost seven straight tarpon before finally landing one. The following morning, they left Fort Jefferson for the ten-hour cruise back to Key West. The weather conditions that had sent Thompson back early presented no problems for Captain Bra.

By the end of May, all of the out-of-town Mobsters had left on the FEC train out of Key West. Ernest figured it was time for Paul Pfeiffer and him to join Pauline in Piggott, Arkansas, a fourteen-hundred-mile drive. Before leaving, he asked Lorine to find a house for Pauline and him for the next season of 1929. She didn't think he was serious about it.

In late May 1928, leaving Key West by automobile was no easy task. Although the railroad had been in place since 1912, U.S.1, the Overseas Highway, was missing a few stretches of pavement. They drove to No Name Key, where Ernest had met Georgie Brooks. From there they took the 9 A.M. ferry to Lower Matecumbe Key, a five-hour trip covering some forty-one miles. From the town of Islamorada, they picked up U.S. 1 and drove across concrete and rickety wooden bridges, finally crossing a long, wooden bridge at Ocean Reef. They arrived at Florida City on the mainland just before sunset.

The next time Hemingway returned to Key West, in the fall of

1928, he would bring with him a new baby. After an eighteen-hour labor, Pauline had delivered Patrick Hemingway, a nine-and-a-half-pound boy, in Kansas City, Missouri, on June 28, 1928.

❖

CHAPTER IV

❖ ❖ ❖ ❖ ❖ ❖ ❖ ❖ ❖ ❖ ❖

THE HOUSE ON WHITEHEAD STREET

"FIND US A HOUSE FOR NEXT WINTER." That's what the Hemingways had asked Lorine Thompson. Then they had left for Kansas City, where Pauline would give birth to their first child. Charles Thompson did not expect them to return.

"It was fun but we've seen the last of that gang," he said sadly.

Charles was wrong. They came back a second and then a third time. Then in 1930 Ernest told Charles he would like to look around Key West for "a place to hang my hat." Nothing came of it, probably because he and Charles were more skilled in hunting down sailfish than houses.

What they didn't know was that Lorine had already shown Pauline a big, two-story, rundown stone house at 907 Whitehead Street, set on a scrubbily landscaped acre and a half. "A miserable wreck of a house," Lorine called it. To Pauline it was "a damned haunted house."

When the Hemingways returned in the spring of 1931, they realized the time had come to settle down in Key West. Pauline's Uncle Gus Pfeiffer, who had already given them a Ford for a wedding present, told his favorite niece he would buy a house for them whenever they were ready.

By now Ernest and Pauline knew what they wanted. Ernest needed a secluded place to write. Pauline wanted a setting with a European flavor. And both agreed they needed plenty of living space. By this time Pauline was pregnant again so they would require a yard where two children could play.

"Well, there's always the haunted house," said Lorine.

They took a second look. This time Pauline saw something different—not the neglect of the past but rather the potential of the future. The old Spanish colonial mansion, built in 1851 by the shipping magnate Asa Tift, was actually a magnificent structure, well-suited for the subtropical world of the island. Uncle Gus sold a few shares in Hudnut and let Sloan's Liniment pay for the house for Ernest and Pauline. It was purchased for $8,000 on April 29, 1931.

"Uncle Gus was a small, nostalgic man, the big wheel in Hudnut's in New York," wrote John Dos Passos. "Stiff with money and having neither chick nor child as the saying was, he lavished attention on his smart pretty nieces. Ernest fascinated him. Hunting, fishing, writing. He wanted to help Ernest do all the things he'd been too busy making money to do."

That night Ernest and Charles celebrated by getting drunk at Josie Russell's speakeasy. The Thompsons were, of course, delighted that their new friends would be settling into Key West permanently. But the next day they were dismayed by Pauline's announcement that work on the house would have to wait till next winter. Within a week, the Hemingways—Ernest, Pauline, and young Patrick, going on three—were on their way to Spain. There Ernest would continue work on a book he was writing on bullfighting. The sport, or art, as some would call it, had enthralled him since he had run with the bulls at Pamplona, then written about the happening in *The Sun Also Rises*.

The Hemingways did not move into the house on Whitehead Street until just before Christmas. It was a difficult time for Pauline. Her second child, Gregory, had been born on November 12, 1931, again in Kansas City by Caesarian section. Her doctor told her she should bear no more children.

The main body of the house they moved into in December was constructed of white coral rock, cut from the property to create a giant hole, which became one of the few basements in south Florida. Heart of white pine was shipped to Key West from Asa Tift's lands in Tifton, Georgia, a town he had helped found. Built in Spanish colonial style, the Tift home had for years been an island showplace. Such was not the case when Uncle Gus forked over his $8,000.

Getting the house into livable condition helped solve some of Key West's dreadful unemployment problems. The house swarmed with out-of-work Conchs, noisily and happily putting the place back in order. The crew turned first to a two-story outbuilding, a carriage house in the rear of the house. The second floor of this building would become the studio where Ernest could write. An iron catwalk was built from his second-story bedroom across to his workroom. He was usually at his writing table by 8 A.M., starting each day with

The house on Whitehead Street, in need of landscaping.   *Florida Photographic Archives*

19

a battery of sharpened pencils. "A seven-pencil morning" was a productive day's work for him.

Cabinetmaker Toby Bruce came all the way from Piggott, Arkansas, to build bookcases for the studio, the first of many construction projects he would perform for Hemingway. Plaster cracks were repaired and the room was repainted a light sea green. Toby located an old gateleg table, which became the author's desk, and a wooden cigarmaker's chair with a wide leather bottom and a narrow leather backpiece.

While the work went on, Hemingway struggled to shut out the noise while he continued writing *Death in the Afternoon*. His studio was soon littered with notes on bullfighting and photographs he would use in the book. Pauline told Lorine his study looked like "a lightly organized waste paper can."

By April 1932, Hemingway was delighted with the progress on the house. He wrote his old friend, the painter Waldo Peirce: "This is a grand house. Do you remember it across from the lighthouse. One that looked like a pretty good Utrillo, somewhere between that and Miro's Farm."

From Hemingway, this was high praise. Joan Miro's painting *The Farm,* displaying a Spanish farmhouse and farmyard, was one of his favorites. He bought it for his first wife, Hadley, as a birthday present, then borrowed it after their divorce and never returned it.

Still recovering from the ordeal of Gregory's Caesarian birth, Pauline spent much of her time in bed. For their first Christmas in their first home, a tree was erected at the foot of her bed.

By midwinter the house on Whitehead Street was becoming a home. The structure had been rewired, the plumbing repaired, ceilings and walls replastered, new wooden floors installed, and the leaky roof fixed. The basement, fourteen feet deep, had been converted into a wine cellar for Ernest's European wines.

During their trips to the continent, the Hemingways had acquired many Spanish antiques. These were shipped to Key West, along with several chandeliers of hand-blown Venetian glass. Eighteenth-century Spanish furniture in the dining room included a dining table, a sideboard, and chairs designed to provide guests with a close and convenient place to hang their swords. At the Hemingways', guests would have been more likely to bring boxing gloves.

Most of the interior furnishings bore Pauline's stamp. Ernest's biggest contribution to the house's decor during the Key West years came from hunting trophies. Impressive heads of various big game animals he had killed in the Rockies and in Africa showed up around the house. A mounted wildebeest, hardly a thing of beauty, hung on the dining room wall. Pauline also supervised the landscaping of the property, including the planting of a banyan tree on the south side of the house.

Meanwhile Toby Bruce was keeping busy building tables, wine racks, and an emperor-sized bed. His work on the house would go on for years. Later he would build a brick wall around the property—partly to discourage nosy sightseers, partly to keep the active Hemingway boys inside.

In 1937 Toby oversaw the construction of the Keys' first swimming pool. Pauline, sensing she was losing Ernest, decided to surprise him with a grand gesture. Since he loved to swim, why not his own private pool in the spacious backyard? It could be ready for him when he returned from his lengthy tour of duty covering the Spanish Civil War.

The hunter home from the hills was not pleased. When he learned that the pool cost $20,000, two and a half times the purchase price of the house, he took a penny out of his pocket and flung it to the ground. "You might as well take my last cent," he told her. Retrieving the penny, she had it preserved in cement and covered with glass, much to the delight many decades later of the sightseers Hemingway had hoped to keep at bay.

Saving the penny added a light touch to an absurd scene, but the incident only pointed out one of the reasons their marriage

The famous urinal from Sloppy Joe's.   *Photo by Stuart McIver*

would eventually fall apart. The money Pauline spent on the pool was not Ernest's. Pfeiffer money supported him in style for years. A proud, macho man, he could only have been resentful.

In the lushly landscaped gardens near the pool, a urinal from Sloppy Joe's has been laid out on the ground to serve as a watering trough for the Hemingway cats. Dressed up with tile and a Spanish olive jar, it adds an attractive touch to the scene. And it always brings a snicker from the tourists who have made the Hemingway House and Museum the island's most popular attraction.

❖

CHAPTER V

❖ ❖ ❖ ❖ ❖ ❖ ❖ ❖ ❖ ❖ ❖

THE SPORTING LIFE

HEMINGWAY WAS A SPORTS FAN. He wrote about fishing in the Nick Adams stories; hunting in the *Green Hills of Africa;* bullfighting in *Death in the Afternoon;* baseball and football broadcasting in "The Gambler, the Nun and the Radio;" horse racing in "My Old Man;" and prize-fighting in "Fifty Grand." He hunted in Wyoming, France, and Kenya; fished the freshwater rivers of Michigan and the West and the salt waters of the Gulf Stream and the Caribbean; and boxed wherever he could find a ring and a willing sparring partner. As a spectator, he loved the bullfights in Spain, heavyweight championship boxing matches in New York, and cockfighting in Key West.

Hunting was out of the question in his new hometown since houses and buildings occupied most of the island. But fishing in Florida Bay, the Gulf of Mexico, and the Gulf Stream was superb. And luckily for Ernest, fight night arrived every other Friday.

At the poorly lighted Key West Arena on the northeast corner of Thomas and Petronia Streets, island boxers, mostly blacks, mixed it up before cheering Conchs looking for inexpensive entertainment in the hard times of the Depression. Ringside seats cost $3, general admission to the grandstand, $1.25. The fights usually drew several hundred spectators. Fighters paid from the gate picked up $25–30 a fight.

James "Iron Baby" Roberts, a light heavyweight, was still in his teens when he first saw the celebrated author at the Key West Arena. "Hemingway looked like an ordinary hippie," Iron Baby told Paul Heidelberg, who wrote about the Key West fight scene in *Sports Illustrated*. "I always tell people that it was the first time I saw a hippie, because he used to dress that way. He had a long beard, and he needed a haircut, and he was wearing shorts and an old shirt, just like a common person. You'd never have guessed that he was the big writer he was. He carried right on like everyday people. That's the way he lived here."

That night Hemingway was refereeing the main event, a bout between Alfred "Black Pie" Colebrooks and a talented Cuban fighter with an Anglicized name, Joe Mills. Working in Colebrooks' corner was Kermit "Battling Geech" Forbes, sometimes known as "Shine."

Mills kept belting Black Pie to the canvas, "about eight times," Forbes recalls. Black Pie was game, maybe too game. He kept getting up.

"This is enough," said Shine. He threw in the towel, a signal that Colebrooks' corner wanted the fight awarded to Mills on a technical knockout. Hemingway threw the towel back. Shine threw it back in and back out it came. After the third unsuccessful towel-tossing, Shine jumped into the ring and swung at Hemingway, a futile venture since the author towered more than a half a foot above the enraged Shine.

The furious fighter couldn't reach him. He tried jumping up, but after he swung he fell against Hemingway's chest. The author grabbed him by both ears and shook him. Policeman arrived to arrest Forbes.

"No, don't arrest him," said Hemingway. "Anytime a man's got guts enough to take a punch at me, he's all right."

"I didn't know who he was," Forbes said. "Nobody told me. I thought he was some bum trying to pick up a dollar. When I got

Hemingway Days Festival
"Iron Baby" Roberts, left, and "Shine" Forbes recapture their
glory days as boxers in the 1930s.

home my mother said, 'Do you realize who you just took a punch at?
It was Mr. Ernest Hemingway, the famous writer.' I went over to
Hemingway's house that night to apologize. Hemingway shook my
hand and then challenged me to come over the next day. That's
when our sparring began."

Hemingway set up a boxing ring near the swimming pool in his
backyard. He had two speed-punching bags and one heavy bag and
three kinds of gloves—eight, ten, and sixteen ounces. At one time or
another, all the local fighters sparred with him at fifty cents a round.
All, the story goes, were beaten by him, but, said Iron Baby some
years later, "We all took it easy on Mr. Ernest. We'd go about three or
four rounds with him. I was the only one he was kind of leery of, on
account of my weight. We were pretty young then, and Hemingway
was older than us, but he'd give us a tussle. I didn't wear any headgear, but Hemingway did. Geech didn't wear any headgear, either."

In World War II, Roberts would become a ranking light heavyweight, and Shine Forbes a ranking lightweight in the Army. Black Pie, just fifteen at the time of his losing battle with Mills, later studied music at the Bradley University Conservatory of Music. Iron Baby Roberts later spoke highly of the treatment of blacks by Hemingway and the people of Key West.

"The average person in Key West didn't believe in this segregated stuff with black and white. We all lived next door to each other. We didn't know anything about white sections and black sections. I was raised with white guys; Hemingway was friendly with black people. But the whole town was that way."

One Christmas Hemingway threw a big outdoor party at his Whitehead Street house. Part of the entertainment was a boxing exhibition put on by Roberts, Forbes, and other Key West pugilists. Among the celebrity guests that night was Gene Tunney, former world's heavyweight champion, the boxer who dethroned the great Jack Dempsey. The fighters were paid after the hat was passed. Tunney, the only one of the guests who talked to the fighters, deposited $200 in the hat.

Hemingway's most famous Key West fight occurred outside the ring. In 1936 his sister Ursula arrived at his house in tears. At a cocktail party, the poet Wallace Stevens, visibly drunk, had belittled her brother's writing. On a rainy February night, Hemingway returned with Ursula and confronted the inebriated poet as he was leaving the party. Stevens, a muscular six-foot-two 225-pounder, regarded himself as something of a boxer, although he was a good twenty years older than Ernest. Stevens' best punch missed and Hemingway belted him into a puddle of water in the street. Later, Stevens apologized to Ursula. In the 1950s, both writers would win Pulitzer Prizes, Stevens for poetry, Hemingway for his novel *The Old Man and the Sea*.

Cockfights were held on a large, open lot in the southwestern section of the city, just off Amelia Street. In the center of the lot, a circular area was fenced in to form an arena for the roosters. Bleachers on the north and south sides of the arena provided seats for about a hundred spectators.

Following the Latin tradition of the bullfight, trainers and handlers began to arrive with their fighting cocks, carried in brightly colored cages. Soon a noisy crowd assembled. Cubans and Conchs gathered around the arena, wearing their Sunday best—white suits, loud ties, and Panama hats. Vendors were on hand, selling homemade Popsicles and hot tacos. Homemade wine and Hoover Gold were passed around.

Just before 1 P.M., the big bettors showed up. The wealthiest of the Cubans, usually the *bolita* bankers, and the most affluent of the Conchs and the town's political leaders parked on Emma Street and strutted down Amelia Street to the scene of the action. Promptly at 1:00, handlers faced off following the traditional challenge.

"You want to fight your rooster?"

"Yes, I want to fight my rooster."

The gamebirds were bred and trained to kill. Some sported razor-sharp artificial talons. The length of the match was limited by an hourglass set for fifteen or thirty minutes—or by the death of one of the fighters.

Betting between fans began immediately. Tens of thousands of dollars could change hands on a given Sunday, and none but an expert would be aware of anything happening anywhere except in the arena. Victory came when a rooster was so weakened by pecks or slashes from spurs that he was unable to continue. Usually the fighting cocks died. If not, they were killed. A draw, which meant that no money changed hands, was considered such a disgrace that the shamed roosters had their necks wrung. After the fights, bettors adjourned to motel or hotel rooms or to speakeasies to settle their bets. A winner could pocket as much as $10,000 on a winning Sunday.

Cockfighting was, of course, illegal. Hemingway enjoyed the color and excitement of the sport, conducted within easy walking distance of his home.

❖ ❖ ❖

Despite his love of the sporting life, Hemingway was not always a sporting man. His closest friend, Charles Thompson, was horrified when Ernest shot an eagle on a hunting trip in the Rockies. Poet Archibald MacLeish likewise was disturbed when the novelist shot terns for target practice and let their bodies just drop into the sea.

As a boy of sixteen, Ernest was involved in an illegal shooting incident at Walloon Lake in the summer of 1915. He and his sister Sunny were exploring the lake area. Ernest flushed a blue heron out of the reeds, then shot it. He knew the act was against the law, but he figured the large wading bird would make a handsome addition to his father's collection of stuffed birds.

Unfortunately for young Ernest, game wardens learned that he had killed a protected bird. When they arrived at the Hemingway house, the boy had already fled the area on the advice of his mother. Later that summer his father advised him to come out of hiding and face up to what he had done. He pleaded guilty before a judge and paid a fine of $15.

Ironically, years later in Key West, Ernest often engaged the services of a commercial fisherman and skilled boatman named Morrell Bradley. Morrell, who worked with him aboard *Pilar*, was the oldest son of Guy Morrell Bradley, the first Audubon warden killed in the line of duty. Guy's principal job had been to protect the large wading birds of south Florida, among them blue herons.

❖

CHAPTER VI

❖ ❖ ❖ ❖ ❖ ❖ ❖ ❖ ❖ ❖ ❖

PILAR

NOT SINCE HIS BOYHOOD DAYS on Lake Walloon in northern Michigan, in the land of his Nick Adams stories, had Hemingway had a boat of his own. The time had come for him to move past chartering boats or fishing from one of his friend's boats. The Old Master craved mightily a sportfishing boat that he himself owned outright, named by him and built to his specifications. He had learned enough about the seas around Key West, about the Gulf Stream, to know exactly what he wanted. In the catalogue of the Wheeler Shipyard in Brooklyn, he had found his dream boat—a diesel-powered thirty-eight-footer with twin screws, double rudders, ample bunk space, and the kind of seaworthiness that could stand up to the action of the Gulf Stream. The price for the thirty-eight-footer was $7,500—a lot of money in 1934—but his fortunes were clearly improving.

After his African safari, Hemingway boarded the *Ile de France* to return to New York. There he made two important visits. The first was to *Esquire,* a new men's magazine for which he was already writing. Always a persuasive man, he talked editor Arnold Gingrich into advancing him a hefty $3,300 against future magazine stories. Next, armed with his *Esquire* check, he piled into a cab with Pauline and headed for Brooklyn, to the Wheeler Shipyard. He used the check as a down payment on the boat of his dreams. She would have Wheeler's standard thirty-eight-foot hull, planked with white cedar and framed with steam-bent white oak. The forward cabin would be a double stateroom. In addition, the boat would have a head, two bunks, and a dinette, complete with galley and icebox.

Hemingway added a few touches of his own. He had the stern cut down a foot to reduce the distance a fish had to be lifted to bring it aboard. He planned on reeling in trophy catches. And to make it easier to pull large fish into the cockpit, he had a large wooden roller installed over the transom. Delivery was promised in thirty days, F.O.B. Miami.

He had already picked out the name for his boat. It proved to be one that overjoyed Pauline. One of her little-used nicknames was Pilar. And *Pilar* became the name of one of the world's most famous sportfishing cruisers. Pauline had to share the honor of the name with a Catholic bullfight shrine in Zaragosa, Spain.

Back in Key West, Ernest started to work on the safari book he would call *Green Hills of Africa.* The evening of May 9, 1934, he and Pauline were entertaining a convivial group of guests that included John and Katy Dos Passos, the Thompsons, and Hemingway's nineteen-year-old brother, Leicester, nicknamed the "Baron." Word came that *Pilar* had just arrived by rail in Miami. The party turned even more festive.

The next day Hemingway dropped work on his book. He and Captain Bra Saunders took the afternoon train to Miami to pick up the cruiser. Hemingway and Bra launched *Pilar* into Biscayne Bay and headed south through the Keys. As Ernest stood behind the wheel, he gazed down on a bronze plaque that read:

HULL 576
Wheeler Shipyard
Boat Manufacturers
1934
Brooklyn, New York

Captain Hemingway checks out *Pilar*.   *Monroe County Library*

On *Pilar*'s maiden voyage, a representative from Wheeler traveled with them, checking out the engines, a seventy-five-horsepower Chrysler with a reduction gear to turn a powerful, slow-speed propeller and a forty-horsepower Lycoming for trolling. The boat could do a full sixteen knots on a calm sea.

Captain Hemingway steered *Pilar*, freshly varnished and gleaming with its coat of black paint, into the Key West Navy Yard. He had already obtained permission from the commanding officer to dock his boat there free of charge. The Mob was waiting on the submarine docks. When *Pilar* cruised into the basin, the Mobsters let out a big whoop and blew horns to celebrate the event.

That night glasses were raised to toast the boat Ernest called "the new skiff." Bra was warm in praise of *Pilar*: "Now you boys know somethin' about boats. . . . This one rides so high, lighter than any craft around here, or the Bahama boats or the Cubans either. She whines like her big engine is burnin' up, but it's not. It's the reduction gear."

In his book, *My Brother, Ernest Hemingway*, the Baron gave an eyewitness account of *Pilar*'s shakedown cruise. Pauline had brought hampers of sandwiches, fruit, cold drinks, beer, ice, and paper towels and napkins to keep the scene neat. Ernest trolled the eastern dry rocks, the Sand Key area, the western dry rocks, then back again. They encountered no large billfish but caught a few barracuda and grouper and one amberjack.

The skipper didn't seem to mind. Hemingway was using the first cruise to get the feel of the boat. At a speed of ten knots, he swung *Pilar* into a hard turn to starboard and then to port. Then he opened both engines up and *Pilar,* wrote Leicester, "seemed to plane," throwing back a great wake. Ernest brought his craft up to better than fifteen knots.

Hemingway turned the wheel over to his younger brother and moved around the boat, checking for vibration, feeling the temperatures, testing the engine hatches. He wandered all over the boat to get the feel and the sound of the boat running through the water. "I want to know what she's like all over," he said. The knowledge he gained from the performance of the boat in a wide variety of conditions, the Baron concluded, "proved invaluable in handling the *Pilar* in foul weather."

Near the end of May, Ernest finally boated the kind of fish he had envisioned for *Pilar,* the biggest Atlantic sailfish ever taken on rod and reel. Unfortunately, it could not be claimed as an official world's record.

A visiting Catholic priest from Miami had been invited to fish with Ernest and Leicester. They had cruised out to the Gulf Stream near the Marquesas. By 3:30 that afternoon, they had had little success, but Hemingway was relaxed, well plied with sandwiches and beer.

"Sun and sea air, as they dry your body, make for almost effortless beer consumption," he said. "The body needs liquid of a nourishing kind. The palate craves coolness. The optic nerve delights in the sensation of chill that comes from its nearness to the palate as you swallow. Then the skin suddenly blossoms with thousands of happy beads of perspiration as you quaff."

Suddenly, a cry from Father McGrath broke through the lyrical tribute to beer. The priest had hooked himself a billfish.

"Reel as fast as you can, Father," said Ernest. But a shark took the fish away from him. Soon the priest had hooked another, this one a monster of a sailfish.

"Fight him, Father," called the skipper, maneuvering his *Pilar* skillfully.

Twenty-eight times the fish jumped. Father McGrath, hampered by arthritis in his left hand, tired after some fifteen minutes of trying to hold the mighty leaper.

"Ernest, you must help me. I can't handle this fish any longer."

"Look, he's yours," said Hemingway. "He's a sailfish, not a marlin as I first thought. He may be of record size. If I take over, the fish will be disqualified for any kind of record."

"But I can't go on."

Leicester took the wheel from his brother and Ernest relieved a weary Father McGrath. He battled the fish for nearly three-quarters of an hour. Finally he pulled the fish aboard. It measured over nine feet long and weighed 119½ pounds. For the rest of his life, Hemingway could legitimately claim he had boated the largest Atlantic sailfish ever taken on rod and reel—but he couldn't claim it as an official record. Hemingway docked at Charles Thompson's docks at the foot of Caroline Street. There they strung the giant sailfish up and Hemingway proudly posed for a photograph beside the trophy he—and Father McGrath—had reeled in.

"Toast to the good Father," said Ernest, raising a glass back at the house. It was a gracious gesture, since the handling of the rig by two anglers deprived *Pilar* of a major record in her first month of fishing.

After Father McGrath returned to Miami, he typed out a story about the feat and delivered it, along with the photo of Ernest and the fish, to the *Miami Herald*. One morning Ernest, working on his African book, heard a commotion downstairs. He joined Pauline and Leicester. They showed him the *Herald*. The story ran on page one. It was signed "Eye Witness."

"Now who . . . ?" mused Ernest. "Of all the. . . . I wanted him to take credit for the catch."

The fish, mounted by Al Pflueger's taxidermy firm, hung in the lobby of the Miami Rod and Reed Club, crediting Hemingway with catching the largest Atlantic sailfish ever taken.

"It's their lie, not mine," he told Charles. "Let 'em hang it in their joint."

That year Hemingway enrolled his yacht in the Biscayne Bay Yacht Club, based in Coconut Grove, Miami. It was registered as a thirty-nine-foot cabin cruiser with an eleven-foot beam and a three-foot two-inch draft. Nominated by Norberg Thompson, Charles's older brother, Hemingway had joined the venerable yacht club the previous year. Its members included such eminent boaters as L. H. Baekland, the founder of the plastics industry; Alfred I. DuPont; G. A. Rentschler, founder of Pratt & Whitney Aircraft; Nathanael Herreshoff, one of America's most respected yacht designers; and Arthur Curtis James, reported to be the second richest man in the world. Three of the yachts enrolled at the BBYC exceeded a hundred feet in length. Norberg's boat was the sixty-eight-foot-long cruiser *Mareta*.

Other members included the author Charles Baker, a novelist who wrote regularly for *Esquire,* and Grant Mason, Hemingway's friend from Havana, his base for running Pan American Airways' Caribbean operations. Mason, whom Hemingway once described as a "wealthy twerp," was one of the airline's founders. The Mason Hemingway was friendly with—very friendly with, in fact—was Grant's wife, the gorgeous Jane. Jane was so beautiful that President Calvin Coolidge, who seldom reacted to anything, reacted to her. He called Jane "the likeliest young lady that ever crossed over the threshold in the White House." To Silent Cal, likeliest meant most beautiful.

Why did Hemingway join the Biscayne Bay Yacht Club? His son Patrick later recalled: "There were no clubs in Key West. I remember how delighted he was when he joined the club in Miami." Still,

Miami attorney Thomas Johnston, the club's treasurer during the years of the author's membership, doesn't recall ever seeing him at the club.

For the rest of the spring, Hemingway worked steadily on his safari book, limiting his *Pilar* forays to short cruises in the Key West area. Meanwhile, he began to make plans for his first long trip out into the Gulf Stream. His goal was to spend his thirty-fifth birthday—July 21, 1934—aboard *Pilar* en route to Cuba. His problem lay in assembling a crew capable of heavy-duty sail fishing. For this he needed an experienced captain at the wheel and a mate versed in the difficult task of gaffing large saltwater fish. Hemingway himself had become skillful in handling the wheel, but he wanted more time for fishing.

For mate he sought out Carlos Gutierrez, captain of a Cuban fishing smack. He had known Gutierrez since 1929, when he met

Hemingway, in baseball cap, aboard *Pilar*.   *Sloppy Joe's*

him on a fishing trip to the Dry Tortugas. The fifty-five-year-old Cuban agreed, but that failed to solve the need for a captain. Ernest wanted Joe Russell, but Josie turned him down, a sign of changing times. Josie in recent years had made his living by following two illegal occupations—rumrunner and speakeasy operator. With the coming of Repeal in 1933, Josie went straight. Rum-running was no longer necessary, and the speakeasy had given way to the saloon. Russell's Sloppy Joe's (now Captain Tony's) at 428 Greene Street, three times the size of his tiny Front Street speakeasy, was consuming all his time. Key West was officially bankrupt; still the Conchs imbibed.

"Times might be hard, Cap," Josie told him, "but ol' Mr. Hoover done put a helluva thirst on all the honest folks."

Instead of Sloppy Joe, Hemingway was forced to round out his crew with Charles Lund, a mate on the Key West–Havana ferry, plus two distinguished members from the Academy of Natural Sciences in Philadelphia, Charles M. B. Cadwalader, the director, and Dr. Henry Fowler, chief ichthyologist. He had been corresponding with the academy on research projects involving the marlin.

Off Morro Castle in Havana Harbor, *Pilar*'s larger engine developed trouble. Hemingway anchored offshore while Lund tried to repair the engine. Morro Castle guards, assuming they were gunrunners, sent an armed patrol boat to investigate. As they prepared to board *Pilar*, Carlos shouted to them the magic words, "El Hemingway! El Hemingway." The author was already well known and well liked in Havana. The patrol boat captain apologized and retreated. *Pilar* made it to shore on her trolling engine.

A year later, being well known brought a different kind of reception. Friends tipped Ernest off that local Cuban thieves were planning to loot the boat of the man they viewed as a wealthy American. Around the harbor it was known that *Pilar* was equipped with costly fishing tackle. One night, Hemingway had a friend row out with him to his boat. The friend then rowed back with a sack positioned to look like another passenger. Aboard *Pilar*, Hemingway waited. And waited.

Then he heard the sound of oars in the water. *Pilar* lurched slightly as the intruder stepped aboard. When a dark figure loomed in the cockpit, Hemingway fired a Colt .45 pistol. Next, he heard a splash in the water below. After that, no more intruders.

❖ ❖ ❖

On a 1932 fishing trip to Cuba, Hemingway began the practice of keeping a ship's log, filled with details on weather, boating and fishing conditions, and weights and measurements of fish caught. He was cruising then, not on *Pilar*, but on Sloppy Joe Russell's *Anita*. In one sense it was a casual exercise since he used a pad of Western Union cable blanks to record his daily notes, but there was nothing casual about Ernest's intense concern with learning the art of deep-sea fishing. These notes included priceless information from Carlos Gutierrez on the behavior of big marlin and tuna and on the tactics needed to catch them. William Braasch Watson, professor of modern European history at the Massachusetts Institute of Technology, discovered ten 1930s' fishing logs among the "Other Materials" in the Ernest Hemingway Collection at the John F. Kennedy Presidential Library in Boston.

His 1934 *Pilar* log is particularly intriguing. "Indeed, the log assumes an intricate and sustained narrative . . . complete with plot, characters, a protagonist (Hemingway), atmospheric coloring, and emotional heightening," writes Linda Patterson Miller, professor of English at Penn State University in Abington.

On that trip, an aspiring young writer named Arnold Samuelson served as a rather bumbling crewmember. Or, as Hemingway described him, ". . . slow where he should be agile, seeming sometimes to have four feet instead of two feet and two hands, nervous under excitement, and with an incurable tendency toward sea-sickness and a peasant reluctance to take orders." If he seems rather unkind to Arnold, such was far from the case. Ernest was actually mentoring the young writer, and involving Arnold in keeping the ship's log was part of his training. Hemingway would fire off his observations and Arnold would record them, referring to Ernest as E.H. and himself as A.S. Hemingway's nickname for him was Maestro, sometimes shortened to Mice.

For example, on the fine points of bluewater fishing, Arnold jotted down Hemingway's wry observation on the misguided taking aboard of a still-active, 250–300-pound tiger shark on September 19, 1934: "Finally gaffed him, shot him and on account of him being worth $2, brought him on board, much to the detriment of the boat."

Two days later, "south wind, squally weather" kept Ernest away from his fishing. Result: "E.H. stayed in to work. Did 13 pages." The following day's entries showed Hemingway still hard at work: "Hurricane has gone off north of the Bahamas. . . . E.H. worked A.M. Wrote four pages." The work Arnold was referring to was *Green Hills of Africa.* On September 25, Hemingway completed seven more pages between 6 and 8 A.M. On his six-week voyage through the waters of the Great Blue River, he wrote more than a hundred pages of his book.

Many entries referred to their food aboard *Pilar.* One day the luncheon menu offered "macaroni, salad, alligator pears (avocados), pineapple." Another day it was "macaroni, salad, alligator pears, pineapple." Occasionally lunchtime was a feast, as on September 27, 1934: "pork chops, yellow tail (snapper), salad, alligator pear, melons." A supper listing on the dock at Cuba's Cabanas harbor included fried kingfish, chili, potatoes, green beans, and "macaroni from noon."

Sometimes the log reported the unrest that plagued Cuba in much of the 1930s. On September 2, E.H. "saw 3,000 pounds of dynamite captured in Cojimar." Two days later, he noted "Grau San Martin left yesterday by plane for Miami." The reference was to the sudden departure of Ramon Grau San Martin, a politician who held power only a few months before being forced out by Fulgencio Batista. Three days later he wrote: "Found the streets full of soldiers, constitution guarantee suspended and transportation strike on."

On October 7, Arnold went ashore in Cojimar with Carlos and Bollo, the cook. That night "there was dynamiting in the city and shooting on both sides of the harbor." Arnold, shouting out that night during a nightmare, woke Hemingway, who charged to the forward hatch with pistol drawn. Ernest's comment in the next day's log: "It was fine and cool sleeping on board undisturbed except by dynamiting, shooting and nightmares."

A September 29 entry cast new light on a side of Hemingway criticized by Charles Thompson, unhappy with Ernest for shooting an American eagle, and poet Archibald MacLeish, dismayed at his use of seagulls for target practice at sea: "For the last four days there have been many warblers flying across the Gulf in little bunches of from 6 to 12. Today two passed, looking very tired. One turned to come aboard. E.H. told Carlos (Gutierrez) to catch him as he was afraid he might fly against the glass and hurt himself as we saw them do on the *Paris* coming home from Africa this spring. Carlos missed him, the bird flew off the chart table and after flying very feebly seemed to go down on the water. We headed over and circled but couldn't find him."

In early October, big game appeared. From the October 10 log: "A little after 1 o'clock when lunch was almost ready, Carlos shouted from the bow in great excitement, having seen some fish jump that threw a spray as high as a six inch gun shell bursting in the water. . . . We got in the lines, started the engine and headed for the whales." A half dozen were sighted, "big as submarines," the largest about seventy feet in length, the smallest about twenty five feet. Hemingway fired a harpoon into the head of one of the whales but it pulled loose and no whales were captured that day. Ernest's log comment the next day: "With any luck we should have caught three marlin this week, but as it is all we have is whale stories."

Hemingway's passion for fishing went far beyond simply reeling them in. His interest in the creatures of the sea went so far that

George Reiger, author and authority on saltwater fishing, called Hemingway "The Literary Naturalist." In addition to playing boating host to Cadwalader and Fowler from the Academy of Natural Sciences in Philadelphia, he recorded data in his logs on "scientific fish," his phrase for strange or unrecognizable fish, and, where possible, shipped specimens off to Philadelphia for further study. Arnold, on one occasion, referred to the Academy as "the scientifico."

Disregarding the warning never to eat oysters in any month that lacks the letter R, Hemingway and crew ate a bucket of oysters one day before the arrival of September 1934 near Cabanas, Cuba. One line in the log for August 30 read: "Ate a bucket of oysters, had lunch, caught a few scientific fish and came into Havana harbor."

News about famous literary figures also surfaced in the log. Late in October 1934, "Dos Passos arrived on the United Fruit boat." In January 1935, Max Perkins, Hemingway's famous Scribner's editor, reached Key West. On the 26th, "Max caught a large red grouper and a small one and we caught about 8 mackerel, 9 barracuda and 7 bonito." Two days later, Max caught a thirty-five-pound amberjack and a twenty-nine-pound sailfish.

The most mysterious entry came on September 3, 1934: "Came in, met the coroner's jury, dinner with the Masons (Jane and Grant) and won ten dollars from Mason (unpaid) going into the style of Ruppington. Mrs. M. looking very lovely. M in great form but tired and with dangue (cq) fever. Great deal of wit. The line of demarcation between a deep sigh and a belch is friendship."

Only too clear in the log is Hemingway's increasing anger and frustration when the many errors of fifty-eight-year-old Carlos and the crew cost him major catches. A line would snap, a gaff would fall into the sea, or *Pilar* would accelerate too fast or too slowly. "Carlos gone completely to pot," wrote a perfectionist Hemingway. He was turning away from an old fisherman who had taught him the ways of the Great Blue River—an old fisherman who had told him a true tale of an even older man and a huge fish he fought for days, then lost to the sharks.

40

❖ ❖ ❖

In 1936 the poet Archibald MacLeish had come down to Key West to visit Hemingway. One hot day, the two of them went fishing aboard *Pilar*. But the fish weren't biting and soon the talk became as overheated as the summer air. Ernest grew even angrier when MacLeish told him to "have just another drink and calm down." When they decided to continue the discussion on dry land, Ernest eased the boat into the shallows near a small key between Boca Grande and Snipe Keys. Archie went ashore first. Then Ernest backed out of the shoal waters and gunned *Pilar* for Key West.

When he reached home, Pauline wondered why an angry Ernest was muttering to himself. Finally she learned he had marooned his old friend on an island that belonged to Lower Keys mosquitoes.

"You can't do this, Ernest," she said. "You've got to go back and get him. That's all there is to it. He may be going crazy with the insects, and there's no fresh water on any of these keys."

Pauline insisted that Hemingway go back and rescue Archie. He finally gave in, but relations were never again the same between the two acclaimed writers. Leicester included the anecdote in his book about his brother, but MacLeish later said it never happened.

In the years that lay ahead, Hemingway would accumulate a staggering number of experiences aboard *Pilar*. Perhaps his finest tribute to his storied flagship was contained in a piece he wrote for *Holiday* magazine in July 1949: "She is a really sturdy boat, sweet in any kind of sea."

❖

CHAPTER VII

❖ ❖ ❖ ❖ ❖ ❖ ❖ ❖ ❖ ❖ ❖

THREE FRIENDS
AND A FOE

ERNEST HEMINGWAY WAS A GREGARIOUS MAN. Making friends came easily to him. Keeping them was another matter. If his friends were fellow writers, he eventually saw them as competitors and all too often turned against them. Key West friendships, by their nature noncompetitive, had staying power.

Three Key Westers were particularly close to him: Charles Thompson and Josie Russell, both Conchs, and Toby Bruce, a transplanted Arkansan. A man as opinionated as Hemingway also needed enemies. In Julius Stone he found a worthy foe. Stone for a time was the most powerful man on the island. He was the Kingfish.

THE MIGHTY HUNTER

How could they have been more different—one a tough, intense writer, a bully, and a complex intellectual, the other an uncomplicated small-town shopkeeper, a sweet man with a smile for everyone?

Ernest Hemingway, at times a caricature of the macho man, had to be first in everything he did—hunting, fishing, boxing, writing. All too often, his fierce competitiveness turned him against writer friends he saw as rivals—Gertrude Stein, Sherwood Anderson, John

42

Dos Passos, and F. Scott Fitzgerald.

Charles Thompson—laid-back, easygoing, noncompetitive—fished and hunted just for the fun of it. Free of any needless pressure to prove himself, he just relaxed and outdid Ernest so often it became a source of embarrassment for the writer. Hemingway, never noted for his sportsmanship, took from Charles what he never took from anyone else. He just forced a rueful grin and even dedicated a book on hunting in Africa to his Key West friend and neighbor.

The two met on Hemingway's first day in Key West in April 1928. An avid freshwater fisherman, Ernest began looking for an equally dedicated saltwater fisherman with a boat. He was referred to Thompson, clearly a man with a boat. In fact, the mighty Thompson family, among its many enterprises, owned a fleet of some 125 fishing boats.

Charles's grandfather was a Norwegian who was shipwrecked in the Keys, liked the place, and stayed on to found what would become the largest business empire on the island. He Americanized the family name from Norberg to Thompson. By the time Hemingway arrived in Key West, the Thompsons reigned as the

Photo by Stuart McIver

The Turtle Kraals, one of the many properties of the Thompson family.

43

town's most affluent family. At one time or another they owned and operated Thompson's Docks (now the Land's End Marina); a fleet of fishing boats; a fish processing company; a marine hardware and tackle shop (run by Charles); an icehouse; a cigar box factory; a truck company; a pineapple plantation; a guava jelly factory; and a turtle fishing business that included a fleet of turtle boats, the Granday Canning Company, and the Turtle Kraals.

The Thompsons were a power in the Keys. Charles's oldest brother, Norberg, was elected mayor of Key West in 1915. He also served on the city and county commissions, the Overseas Highway Committee, and the Everglades National Park Commission. Brother Karl was the county sheriff from 1933 to 1941.

The three Thompson boys were all educated in the Northeast. Norberg earned a law degree from New York University. Karl was a graduate of Amherst College in Massachusetts. Charles, who was born in 1898, a year earlier than Hemingway, attended New York City public schools and the Mount Pleasant Military School at Ossining-on-the-Hudson, New York, but not college. He just wasn't as smart as his brothers but was a much nicer man, recalls his old friend Bill Gaiser. "The family recognized it and gave him a less complicated part of the business to run," said Gaiser.

A charter member of the Hemingway Mob, Thompson fished the waters of the Gulf of Mexico, Florida Bay, and the Gulf Stream. When Hemingway traveled to Wyoming to hunt in the spring of 1932, Charles went with him. Both men bagged elks and grizzly bears. It proved to be a warm-up for a much bigger expedition the following year.

In the fall of 1933, Charles joined Ernest and Pauline on the great African safari Hemingway had dreamed of for years. Once again Uncle Gus Pfeiffer, who had bought their car and their house for them, came through with the money for the nine-month trip—a fat $25,000. Charles paid his own way.

Thompson took a steamer from New York to Marseilles, then a

train to Paris. There he was met by Ernest, wearing a black Basque beret and holding a magnum of champagne. The small-town hardware dealer was treated to a grand tour of Paris by a man whose knowledge of the French capital was encyclopedic. In the nearby countryside, the two hunting buddies shot deer and pheasant.

On their final night in France, Ernest, Pauline, and Charles played host to one of the world's most famous and controversial authors, James Joyce. Joyce had written *Ulysses*, an experimental novel too hot to make it past America's prudish censors. Charles, who had already caroused with such literary friends of Hemingway's as John Dos Passos, Archibald MacLeish, and Maxwell Perkins, got drunk that night with the famous Irishman. He later described him as "a grand little man."

From Marseilles, Charles and the Hemingways sailed to Africa. When they disembarked in sweltering heat in Mombasa, Kenya, Hemingway wore a wide-brimmed Stetson, Pauline an ankle-length white dress, and Charles a suit and tie. "Pauline and I looked like missionaries," Charles later recalled. "Ernest had the distinct look of a whiskey drummer."

The train to Nairobi took them past Mount Kilimanjaro. Ernest was so excited, Charles said his grin was "plastered on his face." The excitement the mountain created would surface later in one of the author's most memorable short stories, "The Snows of Kilimanjaro."

For their safari they engaged the services of the most famous of all the African white hunters, Philip Percival. They would later be joined by Percival's partner, the Danish Baron Bror von Blixen, the husband of Isak Dinesen, who wrote *Out of Africa*. Hemingway wrote his own book about his African adventures, *Green Hills of Africa*. In his book Pauline becomes P.O.M.—Poor Old Mama—and Charles emerges as Old Karl, a confusing move since he already had a brother named Karl.

From the start, Thompson outshot Hemingway, not that he was trying to outshine his friend. He simply had better eyesight. They moved south to the Serengeti Plains and celebrated Christmas Day on the shores of Lake Eyasi. Finally Hemingway, after a number of lesser kills, shot a rhinoceros only to learn that Charles had just killed one. In his safari book, he wrote: "We went over. There was the newly severed head of a rhino that was a rhino. He was twice the size of the one I had killed. . . . He had made my rhino look so small that I could never keep him in the same small town where we lived."

Near the end of the hunt, Hemingway killed two giant kudu bulls with magnificent horns at a salt lick near a Masai village. He had redeemed his reputation as a mighty hunter. Or at least he was able to bask in the glow of his triumph for a short while. When he returned to camp, he learned that Charles had bagged one of the largest kudu heads ever taken in East Africa. In his book Hemingway was generous in his praise of Charles: "I was, truly, very fond of him and he was entirely unselfish and altogether self-sacrificing." But, he lamented, "Why does he have to beat me so bloody badly."

Back home again, the warm friendship between Charles and Ernest was soon to face a test far greater than the pressures of an African shootout. Late in December 1936, Hemingway met the author/foreign correspondent Martha Gellhorn in Sloppy Joe's. That meeting would lead eventually to the breakup of Hemingway's second marriage.

As Ernest and Pauline drifted apart, Charles's wife, Lorine, became openly hostile to Ernest, and even Charles for a while became distant in his dealings with his old friend. The Thompsons were small-town, old-fashioned people. They didn't like divorce and they sided with Pauline and the children.

Ernest patched up his relationship with the Thompsons but not with Pauline. The marriage dragged on till Labor Day 1940. Circuit Court Judge George "Kitty" Gomez had received a request to conduct a divorce proceeding on a holiday to avoid publicity. He couldn't believe it when he walked into his Miami courtroom and saw standing before him his old friends, Charles and Lorine Thompson. He thought of them as "as happy a couple as ever married." The Thompsons quickly explained it was a divorce in absentia. They were simply standing in for the Hemingways. Later the judge joked about it with them but they found nothing to laugh about.

On his occasional trips back to Key West from his new home in Cuba, the author continued to call on his old friends. His last visit to them was in 1960. Lorine recalled it: "He was coming through from Cuba on his way West. You know, he usually had a spring in his walk that sort of shook the whole house. But that time, his feet were sort of dragging."

A year later, in Ketchum, Idaho, Hemingway killed himself with a shotgun. Charles made one last visit to his old friend—to attend his funeral.

Charles died on February 18, 1978, in his rambling, rundown house on Seminary Street. His walls were still decorated with the heads of the trophy kills from the African safari, among them the giant kudu that had so embarrassed Hemingway. And so embarrassed Charles.

"It seemed so unfair,' he said. "Ernest was a better hunter and a better shot. But almost every time I shot something bigger. It was just a freak."

SLOPPY JOE

Their friendship was foreordained. Joe Russell had two things essential to Ernest Hemingway's happiness—a charter boat for fishing and a speakeasy for imbibing. If those two elements weren't enough, Josie did Hemingway a favor that endeared him to the author forever.

Not long after he arrived in Key West, Ernest received a royalty check from Charles Scribner's for *A Farewell to Arms*. When the author took the check, for just under a thousand dollars, to the First National Bank, the bank president took one look at Hemingway, and what did he see? A scruffy-looking bum. Definitely not the kind of man who should be bringing in a thousand-dollar check. Too big a risk. He refused to cash it.

Hemingway went next to Sloppy Joe's, Russell's tiny elbow-shaped speakeasy at the corner of Front and Duval Streets. Josie, without hesitation, cashed the check for Ernest. It was a welcome gesture of trust. It also revealed Russell as a successful businessman with a good supply of cash on hand. Hemingway promptly returned to the bank and told President William Porter, "To hell with your bank. I have my own private bank now and I'll get all my checks cashed there from now on."

Russell and Hemingway were fishing buddies from the start, always comfortable with each other. "Josie Grunts," as Ernest called him, was born in Key West in 1890. He had worked for awhile as a cigarmaker until most of the industry moved away to Tampa. Later he opened a speakeasy and bought a boat big enough to fish the waters of the Gulf of Mexico, the Gulf Stream, and the Atlantic.

Combining the enterprise of charter boating with the operation of an illegal saloon, Josie took a logical next step. Instead of buying boot-leg whiskey for his speakeasy, he moved into the rum-running business. He, in effect, eliminated the middleman. Hemingway claimed that the red-faced Conch was the first Key Wester to make the run to Cuba to bring back "Hoover Gold," as Josie called illegal booze.

Russell, who was married and had a son and two daughters, behaved himself in Key West. He seldom drank in his hometown. The high seas and Havana were the two places where he cut loose. He used to tell Hemingway about the fun of marlin fishing off Cuba. "Ernest," he said, "those big fish are the most exciting thing to catch there is."

In April of 1929, Hemingway chartered *Anita*, Josie's thirty-four-foot, sponger-type launch, for half of Russell's usual fee of $20 a day for a trip to Cuba. The outing was planned for two weeks. It lasted two months.

Sloppy Joe Russell raises a toast to a successful day's fishing with
Hemingway.

They rented rooms at the Ambos Mundos Hotel in Havana for
$2 a day. In the mornings they fished for marlin, and in the after-
noons Ernest worked on the galley proofs for *Death in the Afternoon*.
After dark, the nightlife of Havana beckoned—jai alai, seafood,
daiquiris, and the Cuban capital's famed beauties. On his later visits, Ernest had a particular favorite, one Jane Mason. He faced something of a complication with this affair since she was married to a
friend of his, Grant Mason, a major investor in Pan American
Airways.

Jane helped solve the problem of where to meet by coming to
his room at the Ambos Mundos. He later claimed that she would

climb through the transom in her eagerness to join him. Apparently, very few people believed this boast.

"Her grave beauty had a madonna-like quality accentuated by a middle part in smoothed-back blond hair," Ernest's brother Leicester wrote of her. "She had large eyes and fine features."

The "madonna-like quality" that Leicester wrote of was an illusion. In Denis Brian's *The True Gen,* a friend of Jane's says of her: "Jane Mason not only drank a bit, but was one of the wildest, hairiest, most drinking, wenching, sexy superwomen in the world . . ."

Hemingway, who once described Jane's wealthy husband, the handsome Grant, as a "twerp," compared the Masons' marriage to the Russells'. As that old gang of his grew older and more mature,

Florida Photographic Archives

Marlins were big losers to a group of happy and accomplished anglers, left to right, Jane Mason, Ernest Hemingway and Josie Russell.

Ernest lamented his problem in persuading members of his Mob to join him in his ventures without their spouses. He wrote to Dos Passos: "Mrs. Mason is almost as apt at going places without her husband as Mr. Josie is without his wife. But then Mrs. Mason has also had her husband for a long time too although Mr. Josie I believe there is no doubt has had his much much oftener as well as longer than Mr. Mason."

On December 5, 1933, at 5:32 P.M., an event occurred that made Mr. Josie less available for trips to Cuba. The repeal of the Eighteenth Amendment ended Prohibition. Joe Russell promptly moved out of the illegal speakeasy business and into the legal saloon game. He rented a larger bar, called the Blind Pig, from Isaac Wolkowsky for three dollars a week.

The Blind Pig, located on the south side of the 400 block of Greene Street, was a wooden frame building, fully three times as large as the original Sloppy Joe's. Dark and narrow, the bar had no front door. It didn't need one. The bar never closed. Josie operated Sloppy Joe's as a rowdy fisherman's saloon. Hemingway enjoyed observing the "types" who brought the bar a bustling business.

When *Pilar* arrived in Key West the following spring, Ernest invited Josie to accompany him on the new boat's maiden voyage to their old Havana haunts. For the first time, Joe declined a Hemingway invitation to fish. He was serious about making a success of his new bar. He was serious in many ways where Sloppy Joe's was concerned. He and his bartenders were required to always wear blue serge pants, a white shirt, and a tie. Josie always wore a bow tie.

At Sloppy Joe's the price was right, at least by today's standards. Ten beers for a dollar, ten cents for a shot of gin, fifteen cents for a whiskey, and thirty-five cents for the bar's highest priced drink, Scotch and soda. Hemingway, who drank Haig and Haig Pinch Bottle, got his for a quarter, perhaps a volume discount.

On May 5, 1937, Sloppy Joe's moved again, this time just a half block to the southeast corner of Greene and Duval Streets. Josie balked when Wolkowsky decided to raise the rent a dollar a week. Russell had learned that the old Victoria Restaurant building was available. Bigger and better constructed, it featured the longest bar in town. The time has come, Josie reasoned, to own, not rent. He bought the building for $2,500. The move to the new location was spectacular, dramatic, and crafty.

The lease with Wolkowsky had stated that Josie would have to leave behind the many bar appointments he had added in his four years at the Greene Street location. So Joe let the lease expire, figuring that when the clock struck midnight he was no longer beholden to the terms of the document.

Josie recruited a large and effective force of movers. Their pay that night was drinks on the house at the new bar. Just after midnight, the clientele begin picking up furniture and appointments, including the bar, and carrying them the half block to the new Sloppy Joe's. They also carried their drinks, if unfinished.

"Every drunk in town just happened by," Josie's son-in-law, Bill Cates, told Hemingway when he returned from Spain, "and they carried the whole damn place down the street where they got set up for a night of free drinks."

"Only in Key West," replied Ernest. "Only in Key West."

Wolkowsky returned from a trip to find the building at 428 Greene Street a mere shell. He was furious, of course, but his building continued to prosper as a bar site, first as the Duval Club and later as Captain Tony's.

Josie's premier bartender was a three-hundred-pound black named Al Skinner, a man, it was said, with a "Louis Armstrong smile." Joe Russell Jr., said of him: "Skinner was as strong as a mule, could drink like a horse. But he had manners—always put a napkin down with your drink, always there to light your cigarette." Another regular recalled: "Big Skinner was also Joe's hatchet man if there was anything or anyone to take care of. If Josie didn't want somebody around, Big Skinner would make sure." Artist Erik Smith painted a

Photo by Joan McIver

Sloppy Joe's bustles with action at night.

1933 mural of Sloppy Joe's that shows Josie, Hemingway, and Skinner. It still hangs on the walls at Sloppy Joe's.

A hideaway in the back of the saloon, named the Club Room, was used for gambling. Hemingway once said, "I used to be co-owner of Sloppy Joe's. Silent partner, they call it. We had gambling in the back and that's where the real money is." Joe offered music on Saturday nights. Musicians played for tips from the crowd and a quart of whiskey and a bucket of ice water from Josie.

In June of 1941, Josie and Ernest planned to travel from Havana to New York to meet Toby Bruce and Betty Moreno, the future Mrs. Toby Bruce, who was working in New York. They were scheduled to attend a heavyweight championship fight between Joe Louis and Billy Conn at Madison Square Garden.

While in Havana, Josie entered a Cuban hospital for minor surgery. During recovery, he suddenly suffered either a heart attack or a stroke. Just fifty-one, he died unexpectedly at 3 A.M. in the hospital.

Ernest called Toby: "I'm sorry I stood you up but Josie died yesterday."

Though he died in 1941, Joe Russell's name lives on in Key West, in neon, at his bar, Sloppy Joe's.

TOBY

Most people called him Toby. Hemingway called him "Tobes." Scholarly biographies of Hemingway usually list him as either Otto or T. Otto Bruce. His full name was Telly Otto Bruce. Luckily, his initials, T.O.B., gave him a comfortable escape from either Telly or Otto. He answered to the affectionate name Toby. Some describe him as a handyman, others a jack-of-all-trades. You might even call him a true Renaissance man. It was said that he could fix anything.

For the last three decades of his life, Hemingway had an enduring relationship with Toby Bruce. Toby was Hemingway's chauffeur, secretary, and guardian of Ernest's one true and lasting love, the boat *Pilar*. He was a hunter and a fisherman and a movie actor. He was a carpenter and a cabinetmaker. He made the house on Whitehead Street livable, then protected it with a wall and finally added the first swimming pool ever built in the Keys. He bought Hemingway's cars for him, even negotiated the purchase of the author's home in Cuba, then supervised the massive project to convert the Finca into a home where Hemingway could live and work. He wrote letters for Ernest, read galley proofs, and even demonstrated his talent for drawing by designing the dust jacket for *For Whom the Bell Tolls*. After the author's death, he and his wife, Betty, worked with Ernest's widow, Mary, to sort out the vast assortment of Hemingway material found stored at Sloppy Joe's. Through it all Toby was a friend who stayed close to Ernest through three marriages, starting with Pauline.

To Pauline, however, Toby was a servant. His hometown was Piggott, Arkansas, where the Pfeiffers were lords of the realm. Toby's father owned a hardware store and worked too as a mule and horse trader. Toby, who was born June 24, 1910, met Ernest in 1928 on his first visit to Piggott, just prior to Patrick's birth in Kansas City. The author was walking along the street, sporting tattered clothes, a ragged beard, and a burn under one eye. One arm was in a sling. Jeering teenagers tossed rocks at him. They were surprised when he

Dust Jacket for
For Whom the Bell Tolls
was designed by Toby Bruce.

Photo by Stuart McIver

went to the home of Piggott's wealthiest family, even more surprised when he was let in. The teenagers, afraid they had committed a massive blunder, asked Toby, then only eighteen, to apologize for them. When Toby went to the Pfeiffers' home, he was introduced to the "tramp," who turned out to be Pauline's husband.

Toby and Ernest met again when Hemingway returned from Kansas City after Patrick was born. This time the sling was gone, so the two of them went trap shooting together. Six years later, they hunted quail together, and Ernest raised the possibility of Bruce's coming to Key West to work on their house and also to build a brick wall around the Hemingway home. Toby hitchhiked to Key West in early 1935, then stayed on the island most of the rest of his life.

Hemingway had good reason for wanting a wall. He had been furious ever since the city's tourism gurus had listed his house as a tourist attraction—number eighteen on a list of forty-eight. He decided the best way to keep the sightseers at bay was to build a wall.

It was not a simple task. Toby had never built a brick wall and

55

had never before labored in Key West's summer heat. For his building blocks, Toby hoped to use bricks dug up when the city decided to pave its streets with asphalt. A Key West city commissioner, who had no power since the federal government had taken over the bankrupt city, called the wall "an eyesore" and used his influence to "bar the Hemingway crowd" from the city's brick sites. Ernest bypassed the problem by purchasing "old Baltimore" bricks that were stored at the naval facility. Toby borrowed a pickup truck and hauled the bricks to Whitehead Street three thousand at a time. Bruce finished in late August, just before the September hurricane season set in. Toby wasn't sure how good a job he'd done, but Ernest was delighted with the six-foot wall.

"Now that I've gone private," he said to Toby, "they might even take me off the tourist list." It was a split decision. Hemingway's house stayed on the tourist list, but the wall gave him the privacy he had wanted. He set in immediately to read the galley proofs for *Green Hills of Africa.*

Toby's goal had been to complete the job before a hurricane hit the Keys. The wall finished, he set out for Piggott on August 30. Three days later, the most devastating hurricane in Keys' history, the Labor Day hurricane of 1935, hit the Upper Keys. He learned of the terrible storm when he visited a cousin in Evansville, Indiana.

On his return to Key West, Hemingway showed his pleasure with Bruce's work. "Went on the payroll full-time in nineteen thirty-five," said Toby. "Ernest paid me sixty-five dollars a week. Good wages back then."

And what did he do for his money? "Everything. Worked his fishing boat. Built his furniture. Took his glasses off when he'd fall asleep in bed. Drove his car on all his trips. Carried his money. Bought what he needed. Even read proof and corrected the spelling for *For Whom the Bell Tolls.*"

Drawing was another of Toby's many skills. Hemingway had him design the dust jacket for *For Whom the Bell Tolls,* his book about the Spanish Civil War. Bruce sketched out a little village at the foot of a mountain. In the background is the bridge that was blown up. An artist at Scribner's did the finished artwork. Toby treasured a leather-bound copy of the galley-proof sheets. Hemingway had inscribed the book to him: "With much affection and deep appreciation for all he did to make this book—Ernest Hemingway."

When Papa moved away to Cuba, Toby went with him, rejecting Pauline's efforts to hire him herself. Hemingway felt his celebrity status would drive up the price of the property he and Martha Gellhorn wanted to buy. Toby handled the purchase, keeping the famous author out of the proceedings.

Bruce kept in touch with Key West, particularly with one Laura Elizabeth "Betty" Moreno. Pretty Betty, good-natured but feisty, traced her Key West lineage back to her great-grandfather, Benjamin Curry, before the Civil War. She knew Hemingway from the days when he had briefly rented a house across the street from her family home. As a child, she had played with Ernest's oldest son, Jack, better known as Bumby, when he visited his father. "He was a beautiful boy," she recalls of Hemingway's son from his first marriage.

When World War II came, Toby returned to the United States. He worked with the Army Corps of Engineers in California, and Betty took a job as an assembler with Sperry Gyroscope in Brooklyn. They married in New York in 1943.

After the war, the Bruces returned to Key West. Toby opened the Home Appliance Store, an enterprise that made good use of his reputation as a fix-anything man. He continued to visit Hemingway in Cuba, and the Bruces also saw him on his occasional trips back to Key West.

One day at the beach, Betty made friends with a visiting couple. She gave them a tour of Key West, then took them to meet some of her friends. When she introduced the husband as Bud Schubert, he corrected her.

"It's Budd Schulberg," he said. The group instantly recognized him as the author of the acclaimed novel *What Makes Sammy Run* and of the screenplay for the Oscar-winning movie *On the Waterfront*. Schulberg became a close friend of the Bruce family.

Soon Budd was hard at work on another screenplay, this one for *Wind Across the Everglades*, a tale of the plume-hunting days in Florida. Christopher Plummer was cast in the role of the Audubon warden who tries to stop the illegal slaughter of the plume birds, whose feathers were used to decorate women's hats. Burl Ives played the role of Cottonmouth, head of a nefarious gang of poachers, portrayed by such varied performers as heavyweight boxer Tony Galento, jockey Sammy Renick, clown Emmett Kelly, and actor Peter Falk, the future Columbo. Stripper Gypsy Rose Lee was cast as a whorehouse madam, and author MacKinlay Kantor a judge.

Schulberg asked Toby what part he would like. He said he would like to be a bootlegger. So the scriptwriter wrote in the part for him. In the acknowledgments for the book version of the film, shot mostly in Everglades City, Schulberg wrote: ". . . my old fishing and Matusa-rum drinking chum from Key West, Toby Bruce, made his cinematic debut as Joe Bottles."

Budd must have liked Toby's work. For his next film, *A Face in the Crowd*, shot in Piggott, Arkansas, he employed Toby as a technical advisor. The movie featured Andy Griffith in the starring role. Toby's film work with Schulberg clearly qualified him to evaluate another great actor. "He was one of the greatest actors I've ever known," he said of Papa. "Nobody has ever been able to play Hemingway the way Ernest did. And they never will."

THE KINGFISH

The little island of Key West seems hardly large enough to accommodate the two enormous egos that occupied space there in the mid-1930s. One bristled within the hefty frame of an author whose distaste for tourism has not prevented his unforgettable name from becoming totally entwined with the city's latter-day travel trade. The other lived within the arrogant heart of a powerful government official who saved a dying town by transforming it into a tourist's dream and today is almost forgotten in the city he created.

Ernest Hemingway and Julius F. Stone Jr., two of the most powerful men on the island, were not friends. They had a few things in common—remarkable intelligence and mighty wills. They were close to each other in age and Midwestern backgrounds. Stone hailed from Columbus, Ohio, Hemingway from Oak Park, Illinois. On a personal level, each man was used to having his own way. Each could be high-handed and abrasive in his dealings with people, although Ernest wielded a large measure of charm much of the time.

Apart from the chemistry problem, the major clash appears to have been political. Hemingway was raised in a conservative Midwestern, Republican home. He favored as little government as possible. Stone, on the other hand, was a zealous New Deal Democrat, convinced that government could fix society's problems. It turned out that the irritating Stone was right, which probably rankled Hemingway even more.

Stone came to the island in 1934 after a call for help from Florida's governor, David L. Sholtz. The governor had officially declared the bankrupt island a welfare state. Paying jobs were scarce. The cigar and sponge industries had both moved to the Tampa Bay area. The Navy, a fixture since 1832, abandoned its Key West base as did the Coast Guard. Mallory Steamship Lines no longer called at the island, and Henry Flagler's Florida East Coast Railway was in bankruptcy. Its tax base shattered, Key West, once Florida's most affluent city, had sunk five million dollars into debt. The city was unable to pay policemen, firemen, and garbage collectors. Eighty percent of its residents were on welfare. Per capita income was down to $7 a month. No wonder Hemingway called it "the St. Tropez of the Poor."

As southeastern director of the Federal Emergency Relief Administration (FERA), Julius Stone faced the problem of what to do about Key West. Something about the Key West mission appealed mightily to Stone. Possibly it was the lure of unlimited power or maybe the challenge of reviving what had once been America's most prosperous city.

Stone saw abandoned buildings and houses, collapsing piers, streets littered with garbage. He began by organizing relief recipients into the Key West Volunteer Corps, telling them: "Your city is bankrupt, your streets are littered and filthy, your homes are run-down and your industry is gone. We will begin by cleaning up, then we will rebuild." Among his four thousand volunteers was a man of 102.

The Kingfish pondered his options. With $2.5 million he could provide relief, including food and medical care for the needy, for five years. But the problem would remain: no jobs, no tax base. Another option discussed was simply to close down the island and relocate some three thousand families to the mainland, probably Tampa, where there was some hope of jobs. Not workable, he concluded.

The third option was to find some way to rehabilitate the island. The Kingfish gazed out over his realm, and what did he see? Not just garbage and run-down houses. He saw azure waters teeming with fish, brilliant sunsets over the Gulf of Mexico, bougainvillea in bloom, distinctive architecture. He heard the rustle of the trade winds through the coconut palms. The answer jumped out at him: transform Key West into a tourist resort, a touch of the tropics in a temperate zone.

He put his volunteers to work painting and repairing the houses. He even made the renovation pay for itself. The owners retained title to their houses but the Key West Administration rented them out and applied the rent money to the cost of renovation. After the costs were paid off, the rent money then went to the owners.

Nothing in the FERA guidelines provided for his free-wheeling deals, but that didn't slow him down. "I got away with it," he told

The New Yorker magazine years later, "because we were so far off no one knew what we were doing." Stone reveled in the power the job gave him: "With a scratch of my pen I started this work in Key West, and with a scratch of my pen I can stop it—just like that."

In five months, from July to mid-December 1935, Stone's volunteers renovated more than two hundred guest houses; built thatched huts on the beach; painted and cleaned restaurants, bars, and nightclubs; and remodeled the once-elegant Casa Marina Hotel, which had slipped into receivership. Streets were landscaped, and installation of a municipal sewer system followed demolition of the town's outhouses. On Mallory Square, FERA built the Key West Aquarium. Work resumed on the Overseas Highway, and an airline was subsidized to serve a repaired and improved airport. The Kingfish enriched the cultural life of the island by bringing in artists and organizing theater and choral groups.

Stone made sure the nation's press knew about the Key West story. Within a year the improvement was spectacular. In 1935, forty thousand tourists came to Key West. The island's hotels reported an 85 percent increase in guests. Passenger travel into the city increased by 42.5 percent. Unemployment was reduced by two thirds.

Not everything went smoothly. To further his goal of a "tropical Bermuda," Stone began wearing Bermuda shorts to work, hoping to encourage others to follow his lead. Reaction came quickly. One day an individualistic islander showed up for work in his drawers: "If Julius Stone can come to work in his underwear, so can I."

The conservative *Florida Grower*, published in Orlando, wrote: "FERA rule is the rule of fear. No American city is more completely ruled by one man than is this small island city." In the United Press, Harry Ferguson called Stone "the king of a tight little empire. . . . Call it a 'dictatorship,' a 'kingdom within a republic,' or anything you choose."

Hemingway was particularly irritated by a map prepared by FERA listing forty-eight things for a tourist to see in Key West. It

Monroe County Library

Julius Stone, at right, and J.J. Trevor, president of the First National Bank, stand in front of the East Martello Towers Museum and Art Gallery. Its doors were given to the museum by the bank and gratefully accepted by the Kingfish as president of the Key West Art and Historical Society.

included such memorable attractions as the Sponge Lofts, the Ice Factory, the new Tropical Open Air Aquarium, and the Turtle Crawl, owned by Charles Thompson's family. Number eighteen on the list was Hemingway's home. Gawkers trying to peer into his home disturbed him so much he hired Toby Bruce to build a six-foot brick wall around his place. In a piece called "The Sights of Whitehead Street: A Key West Letter" in *Esquire*, he even reported that visitors, thinking they were visiting an official attraction, occasionally worked their way into his home.

Hemingway's wrath showed in a letter in which he referred to Stone as "that damned Jew administrator," as well as in numerous references in *To Have and Have Not*. One of his characters in his Key

West novel sees an unattractive woman and comments, "Anyone would have to be a writer or a FERA man to have a wife like that." Another character complains that Conchs cannot eat "working here in Key West for the government for six and a half (dollars) a week," overlooking the fact that before Stone's arrival the average per capita income was seven dollars a month.

The heavy hand of Stone's administration was too much for Hemingway. Even with solid accomplishments, Stone was unable to overcome Ernest's opposition to government intrusion. There is a degree of selfishness too in the author's attitude. He was opposed to tourism because an obscure, run-down town gave him more freedom to work. The plight of Conchs out of work seems not to have touched him, perhaps because he knew no want. After all, he had married a rich woman.

Stone moved on in 1937 to study law at Harvard University, where he had previously earned a Ph.D. in organic chemistry. He would later return to Key West and practice law on such a freewheeling basis that he had to flee the country to escape prosecution. Like Hemingway, he lived for awhile in Cuba but there is no indication that their paths crossed there. Both, however, had to flee the island when Castro came into power. Stone died in 1967 in New South Wales, Australia.

Even after their deaths in the 1960s, the lives of these two monstrous egos continued to be intertwined. Stone, to Hemingway's dismay, had converted Key West into a tourism destination. It was moving up in popularity when World War II interrupted. After the war, it became a vacation home for President Harry Truman, who first made Key West a household name in America. It remained, ironically, for Ernest Hemingway, two decades after his death, to fulfill Julius Stone's dream of Key West as one of America's most desirable tourist destinations.

❖

CHAPTER VIII

❖ ❖ ❖ ❖ ❖ ❖ ❖ ❖ ❖ ❖ ❖

HEMINGWAY'S HURRICANE

PAPA HEMINGWAY FIRST HEARD ABOUT THE STORM on Saturday night. He was sitting on the porch, having a drink and reading the evening paper. East of Long Island in the Bahamas, the hurricane on its current track was headed toward the Keys. It was news that was just alarming enough to disrupt his routine, but not quite alarming enough for panic.

Hemingway studied his storm chart, showing tracks and dates of forty September hurricanes since 1900. Using the speed of the storm in the Weather Bureau Advisory, he calculated the probable arrival time for the storm. No sooner than noon Monday, if it hit Key West at all.

Though he was an early riser, the next morning he found a line of boat owners already ahead of him, waiting to have their boats hauled out on the ways, an inclined structure for launching boats. He had to settle for $52 worth of heavy hawser to tie down *Pilar* in what he thought would be the safest part of the submarine base. He secured his boat before he turned his attention to his home.

On the morning of Labor Day 1935, the *Miami Herald*, quoting the U.S. Weather Bureau, referred to the storm only as a "tropical disturbance." Still, it was clear enough by now that the time had

come to board up the house. This was not just a "tropical disturbance." This was clearly a hurricane. Hemingway and his help
nailed up the hurricane shutters and moved outside furniture into
the house. By 5:00 that afternoon, the wind was blowing hard and
steadily from the northeast.

Ernest checked on his boat again, alarmed now that the Coast
Guard had tied up a confiscated booze boat next to *Pilar*.

"For Christ's sake, you know those lousy ringbolts will pull out
of her stem and then she'll come down on us."

"If she does, you can cut her loose or sink her."

"Sure, and maybe we can't get to her, too. What's the use of let-
ting a piece of junk like that sink a good boat."

Back on Whitehead Street, the Hemingways hunkered down.
Ernest figured the storm would hit at midnight. He tried to get a little sleep, placing a barometer and a flashlight by his bed to prepare

Monument to victims of the 1935
hurricane, in Islamorada.

Photo by Stuart McIver

for the inevitable loss of electricity. At midnight the wind was howling and the barometer had dropped to 29.55. He got up and dressed, then decided to go check on *Pilar*. His car wouldn't start, drowned out by the sheets of rain. On his way to the sub yard, Hemingway's flashlight shorted out. When he reached the Navy yard, he saw the problem he had feared. The storm had blown the booze boat's ringbolts out. But the day was saved when a Spanish sailor, Jose Rodriguez, stepped in quickly and maneuvered the boat away from Ernest's craft.

What a storm! Ernest brooded. "You feel like hell," he wrote. "You figure if we get the hurricane from there (the northwest) you will lose the boat and you will never have enough money to get another."

By 2:00 A.M. he noticed a change. The worst of the winds had passed. By 5:00 the barometer was beginning to hold steady. Ernest began to work his way back home in the darkness just before dawn. He found a tree across the walkway to his house. He noticed a strange, empty look in his front yard, and then he saw the reason. The old sapodilla tree had blown down.

Pilar had weathered the storm and, except for a few lost trees and branches, his property on Whitehead Street had come through in good shape. It was time to turn in. The next day, Tuesday, Key West was an isolated world. No communication with the outside world, no boats able to get in or out, no trains able to make it down the FEC tracks.

On Wednesday, a boat from Key West finally reached Matecumbe Key. The news it brought back was horrifying. The hurricane was a small one with an eye only ten miles across. But it proved to be the most intense hurricane ever to strike the western hemisphere. Barometric pressure dropped to 26–35 inches, the lowest reading ever recorded. Wind gauges blew away. Estimates put the wind velocity at 250 miles per hour. A wall of water eighteen feet high swept over Matecumbe Key. Thirty-five miles of railroad tracks were washed away. No train would ever again reach Key West.

It was not, however, the destruction of property that sickened the Conchs. The loss of life was staggering: nearly six hundred fatalities. Whole extended families of old-time Conchs were wiped out. Even more shocking to the nation was the death of some two hundred veterans of World War I. The men had been given temporary relief jobs working on the Overseas Highway that would one day connect Key West with the mainland. The death of the veterans infuriated Hemingway and led to one of the angriest pieces of writing he ever composed.

Hemingway had gotten to know some of the men in the bars of Key West. The veterans were a mixture: some damaged mentally and physically by the war, others just unable to find a job in the depths of the worst depression the country had ever known. The one thing they all had in common was service in World War I, a duty that Hemingway respected deeply.

As soon as the seas would permit, Papa recruited Bra Saunders and Sully Sullivan as crew for a trip up to Islamorada to see for himself. He wrote of finding bodies floating in the ferry slip at Lower Matecumbe, others in mangroves behind tank cars and the water towers, still others high in nearby trees, where the huge hurricane surge had swept them. Some of the victims were people he knew, among them the two likable young women who ran a sandwich shop and filling station.

In an angry article, the author, no friend of the New Deal, blamed the federal government for sending veterans down to the Florida Keys and then leaving them there during the hurricane months. Hemingway implied that the veterans had been placed in harm's way because they were politically embarrassing.

Actually, confusion, blunder, and incompetence were the enemies of the veterans, not an evil conspiracy. Hurricane forecasting had not come of age. Not even the Weather Bureau knew how terrible the storm would be. An evacuation plan had been in place to move the veterans out in an emergency, but the train to be used was not available until it was too late.

The final twist to his story was Hemingway's choice of the publication for his work. The story was published on September 17, 1935, in *The New Masses*, a publication of the American Communist Party. The magazine had contacted him to write the piece and he agreed. He did not particularly like the publication, but it met a need. Ernest Hemingway, angry young man, had a story he had to get off his chest.

❖

CHAPTER IX

❖ ❖ ❖ ❖ ❖ ❖ ❖ ❖ ❖ ❖ ❖

THE KEY WEST BOOK

HEMINGWAY SPENT VERY LITTLE of his adult life in the country of his birth. He wrote a number of superb short stories set in America, many of them in Michigan, where he spent his summers, but he wrote just one novel about life in the United States. For that novel he picked as his book's setting just about the most unrepresentative city in America. Key West is just not like any other place. He wrote about it simply because it was the one town he knew.

Estate of Leicester Hemingway
Ernest Hemingway takes time off from work to relax on his patio.

He called his Key West book *To Have and Have Not*, a title reflecting the contrast between those who have and those who have not, a relevant theme in those Depression years. Unfortunately, it was not one of his best books, a pity since Key West was a locale in which he spent a productive decade, writing all or parts of several books and some of his best short stories.

The book is at its best when capturing the look and the feel of Key West during troubled times. Hemingway depicts the lives of struggling commercial fishermen, charter boat operators, saloon keepers, and veterans working on relief projects in the Keys. The author shows the reader a town deep in the woes of the Great Depression, a town of undernourished people trying to make it through the thirties on "grits and grunts." He wrote of unpaved alleys, Cuban *bolito* parlors, the black-domed bulk of a convent, and a brightly lit main street with drug stores, a music store, "five Jew stores," pool rooms, barbershops, beer joints, ice cream parlors, and six restaurants, five of which he rated as poor, just one as a good place to eat. His was not the glamorized picture of Key West that his foe, Julius Stone, would have liked the world to see. Still, given the high level of unemployment that plagued the island then, the author's insights still ring true many years later.

Hemingway's hero is Harry Morgan, a charter boat captain at a time when the Great Depression dragged the deep-sea fishing business down into the depths. A series of cruel breaks force him to resort to such illegal ventures as rum-running and smuggling illegal aliens. Hemingway drew so heavily on real people that a fear of libel suits induced him to invite Arnold Gingrich and Scribner's lawyer, Maurice "Moe" Speiser, to join him in Key West. They reviewed the manuscript for possible trouble spots.

Gingrich was the man who had suggested that Hemingway write the novel. Ernest had already written two long short stories about Harry Morgan, one of which ran in *Esquire*, the other in *Cosmopolitan*. By adding a third long story and weaving them together, a short novel would result, reasoned Gingrich. Unfortunately, the three separate pieces never quite came together.

When he read the completed manuscript, the *Esquire* editor was treated to an uncomfortable jolt. One of the characters, the novelist James MacWhalsey, was based somewhat on Gingrich, no particular problem since the portrait is actually a likeable one. The problem lay with the character Helene Bradley, clearly patterned after Jane Mason.

At Bimini, Hemingway had introduced Arnold to the beauteous Jane. Within a few months, a smitten Gingrich was seeing her secretly in New York; eventually they married. Arnold suggested to Ernest that Jane and Grant Mason were being "libeled right up to their eyebrows."

"Goddam editor comes down to Bimini and sees a blonde and he hasn't been the same since," teased Hemingway, who obviously knew of the affair.

In the final section that Ernest had written, Grant Mason is depicted as Tommy Bradley, an impotent playboy, and Jane as his nymphomaniac wife, Helene, who collects writers. Since Bradley can't satisfy Helene, he leaves her free to sport with anyone she wishes as long as he gets to watch on occasion.

This would not have made for easy reading for Gingrich. The Scribner's attorney was not happy with it either. He insisted on a strong, though clearly untrue, disclaimer in the front of the book: "In view of a recent tendency to identify characters in fiction with real people, it seems proper to state that there are no real people in this volume: both the characters and their names are fictitious. If the name of any living person has been used, the use was purely accidental."

In addition, Gingrich's remarks were heeded to some extent. Some passages were slightly sanitized. Still, the disclaimer didn't work. It became a popular pastime to figure out who the characters were in real life.

In *Papa: Hemingway in Key West,* author James McLendon presents his rogues' gallery of characters. The book's lead, Harry Morgan, a name adopted from the famed English pirate, is based loosely on Josie Russell, who works overtime as the additional inspiration for Freddy Wallace, the owner of Freddy's Bar, which of course is Sloppy Joe's. Harry's boat, *Queen Conch,* is Josie's *Anita.* Eddy Marshall, a rummy who serves as Harry's first mate, is based on Joe Lowe, a local fisherman killed in the 1935 hurricane.

The Key West States Attorney, George Brooks, whom Hemingway met on his first day in Key West, becomes Bee-Lips, also an attorney. The strange nickname grew out of the way he wrapped his lips around a cigarette. Captain Bra Saunders appears in the book as charter boat captain Willie Adams, a crusty but sympathetic character, "an old man in a felt hat and a windbreaker."

Captain Willie tries to protect Harry from the wrath of Frederick Harrison, a stiff, arrogant, insensitive government administrator. Harrison swears out an affidavit that deprives Morgan of the boat he needs to make a living. When he describes himself as "one of the three most important men in the United States today," it seems clear enough that Ernest is throwing a barb at Julius Stone, the high-handed "Kingfish" of Key West.

An unflattering portrait of a writer named James Laughlin and his wife is based on Mr. and Mrs. Jack Coles, friends of John Dos Passos. By now the friendship between Dos Passos and Hemingway was beginning to collapse. Ernest had difficulty when writer friends achieved high success. At a time when Hemingway's reviews were less than complimentary, Dos Passos was drawing raves for his *The Big Money,* part two in what would eventually become his classic trilogy, *U.S.A.* Acclaim which particularly galled Hemingway was a glowing cover story in *Time* magazine. Only four other American authors had had their pictures on the cover of *Time.*

Ernest struck back at his old friend by basing the character Richard Gordon on Dos Passos. He is presented as a successful but shallow novelist. He is one of the writers ensnared by the charms—and the availability—of Helene. Unfortunately, Tommy peeks in to watch them in the act and Richard understandably goes limp. Helene slaps him twice, then snarls: "So that's the kind of man you are. I thought you were a man of the world. Get out of here."

Gordon's wife, Helen, decides to break up with him and hurls at him what is meant to be a withering insult, "You writer." Is it Dos Passos being insulted? Or is it a case of self-loathing? Could Hemingway really have liked what he was doing to a man who had been a good friend before he became too successful in Hemingway's chosen field? Ernest had become an unhappy man, his marriage falling apart, his recent books poorly received by many critics. He disliked what the New Deal was doing to his Florida Keys and he was shaken by events in his beloved Spain. There the Fascists he hated were seeking to overthrow the country's first democratic government.

Jeffrey Lynn, author of *Hemingway*, a biography that won the Los Angeles Times Book Award, identifies Helen as a somewhat disguised Pauline. Helen is a Catholic, as was Pauline, and she speaks with abhorrence of birth control devices and abortion. Hers is a troubled Catholic conscience and hers is the withering "You writer." Who knows what frictions were developing in the Hemingways' marriage? What is known is that the marriage was beginning to unravel and a terrible sadness was beginning to claim both of them.

It is ironic that *To Have and Have Not*, Hemingway's only book set in Key West, turned out to be one of his lesser works. His time on the island was actually one of his most productive periods. While living in Key West, he completed one of his greatest novels, *A Farewell to Arms*, and worked on another, *For Whom the Bell Tolls*. He wrote his bullfighting opus, *Death in the Afternoon*, and a novelized account of his safari, *Green Hills of Africa*. Hemingway even brought the Spanish Civil War to Key West, where he completed revisions on *The Fifth Column*, his only play, and worked on the script for a documentary film, *The Spanish Earth*. Among the short stories he wrote in

Two of the books Hemingway wrote in Key West.

Photo by Stuart McIver

Key West were "The Short Happy Life of Francis Macomber," "The Snows of Kilimanjaro," "Hills Like White Elephants," and "God Rest Ye Merry, Gentlemen." He used an account Captain Bra told him about the shipwreck of the Spanish liner *Val Banera* as a springboard for "After the Storm," his first story based in Florida.

From his experiences and contacts in Key West, Hemingway drew inspiration for a book that he would not write until the early 1950s. In the Dry Tortugas, McLendon writes, he observed Bra Saunders' gnarled hands beginning to freeze up on him. He saw the sadness in the old fisherman's eyes as he faced the day when his hands would no longer work for him. Two decades later, these hands, concludes McLendon, would become the hands of Santiago, an old Cuban fisherman, based on two Hispanic boatmen Ernest first met in his Key West years—Carlos Gutierrez and Gregorio Fuentes. *The Old Man and the Sea*, Santiago's story, would emerge as one of the best of all Hemingway's novels, reclaiming for him his lofty perch in the world of letters. The book won for him the 1953 Pulitzer Prize and contributed strongly to the Nobel Prize he won in 1954 "for his mastery of the art of narrative, most recently demonstrated in *The Old Man and the Sea*, and for the influence that he has exerted on contemporary style."

❖

CHAPTER X

❖ ❖ ❖ ❖ ❖ ❖ ❖ ❖ ❖ ❖ ❖

PAULINE AND THE BOYS

KEY WEST BELONGED TO HEMINGWAY, first in the '30s when he lived there and again after his death in 1961. But there was a period after he left and moved to Cuba when the Hemingway the island took to its heart was not Ernest but rather Pauline. When their marriage finally broke apart, it was Pauline the Conchs sided with. Long after he left, she stayed on in Key West, operating a business, maintaining the house, and, most important of all, raising their children.

Pauline Pfeiffer, who was four years older than Ernest, grew up in the small rural town of Piggott in the far northeastern corner of Arkansas, not far from St. Louis, Missouri, from which the Pfeiffers hailed. Her family became the power structure of Piggott. Paul Pfeiffer, her father, who had made a small fortune with a chain of drug stores, owned sixty thousand acres of farmland, the cotton gin, and the bank in Piggott. Her uncles in St. Louis, among them the generous Gus, owned the controlling interest in the Richard Hudnut Company, a cosmetics and pharmaceuticals company that included among its products the well-known rub Sloan's Liniment. Pauline was raised in an intensely religious atmosphere. Her mother was a devout Catholic. The Pfeiffers' sprawling white frame house included a chapel.

The future Mrs. Hemingway majored in journalism at the University of Missouri, then went to work at newspapers in Cleveland and New York before becoming a fashion reporter for *Vanity Fair* magazine. Her next move was to Paris, where her fashion writing skills led to the post of assistant to the editor of *Vogue*. In Paris she met Ernest. He was married at the time to Hadley Richardson, the first of his four wives.

Pauline was attracted to the tall, handsome, and already famous writer she saw in the cafes of Montparnasse. He in turn began to notice the slender, shapely woman with dark brown, sometimes impish eyes and stylishly bobbed hair. The attraction grew into a love affair that brought painful remorse to both of them. All his life, Hemingway held a deep love for Hadley, and Pauline, a friend of Hadley's, was a devoutly religious woman. She regarded extramarital sex as a sin, made even worse by adultery.

In January 1927, Hadley divorced Hemingway on grounds of desertion. Ernest and Pauline were married on May 10 in a Catholic ceremony in the fashionable Parisian church of St-Honore-d'Eykau in the Place Victor-Hugo. The bride, always stylish, wore a silk dress and a single strand of pearls. She induced the ofttimes casual groom to wear a three-piece tweed suit and button-down shirt. Raised as a Congregationalist, Hemingway now professed to be a Catholic, using questionable claims to satisfy the qualms of the Church. In time, he would become what some Key West friends called a good Catholic.

By the time the couple first set foot in Key West a year later, Pauline was already pregnant. On her first visit she met Lorine Thompson, Charles's wife. Lorine would remain one of her closest friends for the rest of her life. Pauline did not want her baby born on a run-down tropical island. The Hemingways headed west and on June 27, 1928, labor pains sent Pauline to Research Hospital in Kansas City. Eighteen hours later, nine-and-a-half-pound Patrick was born by Caesarean section. It was a difficult labor, so difficult that her doctor warned that she must not become pregnant again for at least three years.

Just a little over three years later, Pauline returned to Research Hospital for a second time. Again a long and difficult labor, again Caesarian section. The nine-pound baby was named Gregory Hancock Hemingway. He was the third son of the author. Unfortunately, Ernest had wanted a daughter, "a little Pilar," as Pauline once put it.

Pauline was still weak when the Hemingways started the fourteen-hundred-mile trip back to Key West. They moved into the house at 907 Whitehead Street just six days before Christmas 1931. As Christmas approached, the house was a mess, crawling with workers struggling valiantly to make it livable.

Young Patrick, aged three, created true chaos. He mixed a toxic potion in a spray can and then sprayed the baby. Crisis number one. Crisis number two followed when he ate an ant-repellent pellet laced with arsenic. He vomited for the next twenty-four hours. In the confusion that followed, Patrick's French nurse, Gabrielle, became sick and Ernest developed a severe sore throat. Merry Christmas at Whitehead Street.

Isabelle, a spirited black woman, was hired to cook the meals that Ernest, always a zestful eater, needed for his energetic lifestyle. Ada Stern, an aptly named disciplinarian from Syracuse, New York, was engaged as housekeeper and placed in charge of the boys. "An odd sort of Prussian governess," Gregory called her.

When he was seven, Ernest took Patrick to St. Joseph's School, a large wooden school on Simonton Street, where he started first grade. Young Patrick brought home a D in mathematics and for two years was unable to improve his math grade. Two years later, Gregory would enter the same school. Once, after Hemingway had returned from Spain, Gregory showed him *Ferdinand the Bull*, a children's book that particularly delighted him.

"That goddam kids' book has made ten times more than *Death*

Young Gregory Hemingway and housekeeper Ada Stern, a tough disciplinarian for the Hemingway sons.

in the Afternoon," said Ernest. "I worked harder on *Death in the Afternoon* than on any other book in my life and that jerk who wrote *Ferdinand* might have spent a month on it."

Arthur Valladares, whose father owned the town's principal book store, played with the boys after school. He particularly enjoyed romping in their swimming pool. Young Arthur was on good terms with Ernest. He delivered his New York newspapers to him.

The boys were not raised in the happiest of homes. They ate their meals not with their parents but in a small room that adjoined the dining room. By the mid-1930s, their parents were moving inexorably toward the divorce that finally came in 1940. Old-fashioned, small-town people, the islanders generally sided with her. They didn't exactly favor such high-society concepts as breaking up a family with small children. Pauline continued to live in Key West. She and Lorine Thompson went into business together, operating a drapery and upholstering store on Caroline Street.

In 1947, Patrick and Gregory were involved in an automobile accident in a small Crosley car that Pauline owned. Patrick bumped

Hemingway with sons Patrick and John.

his head but the injury did not appear to be serious. Soon after the accident, he visited his father in Cuba. There at the Finca, Hemingway's home, he went into a violent delirium. Ernest personally cared for his son, helping him eat and sleeping just outside his room in the event of troubles during the night. Three months elapsed before he finally recovered. Patrick would later move to Tanganyika, where he owned a three-thousand-acre range. In time he would become a professional white hunter, a calling his father wrote about in books and short stories.

Gregory would eventually study medicine at the University of Miami and go on to pursue a medical career. For awhile, though, he had to work his way through serious problems. In the summer of 1951, he was living in southern California and working in an aircraft factory. A drug problem led to his arrest. His mother, in San Francisco at the time, flew down to Los Angeles to try to help him. That night she telephoned Ernest from the home of her sister, Ginny. His sarcastic remarks unhinged her. She broke into shouting and sobbing at his unsympathetic attitude. That night she awoke at 1:00 with severe abdominal pain. Three hours later, she died on the operating table at St.Vincent's Hospital. She was just fifty-six. Ernest wrote Charles Scribner: "I loved her very much for many years and the hell with her faults."

Some months later, Gregory visited his father in Cuba. When his son mentioned the arrest, Ernest said, "Well, it killed your mother." After medical school, Gregory obtained a copy of Pauline's autopsy. He learned that she had died of a rare tumor of the adrenal gland that had "fired off" apparently due not to the arrest but to the savage phone conversation. He wrote his father, setting the record straight, but the two never saw each other again.

❖

CHAPTER XI

❖ ❖ ❖ ❖ ❖ ❖ ❖ ❖ ❖ ❖ ❖

FAREWELL TO KEY WEST

IN LATE DECEMBER 1936, Charles and Lorine Thompson arrived at Whitehead Street for dinner with Ernest and Pauline. It was a perfect Key West evening—soothing breeze off the ocean, temperature at 70°. Pauline, though, was uneasy with the drift of things. For one thing, she was worried about the North American Newspaper Alliance's offer to Ernest. The Alliance wanted him to cover the war in Spain for the news service, a task that would not only place him in harm's way but at the very least would remove him from Key West for long periods just as she was struggling to hold their marriage together.

She and the Thompsons relaxed with drinks until 7:30, the usual dinner hour. Then Pauline, clearly edgy, said, "Oh, Charles, you know where he is. Drag him back here and let's eat."

Charles knew exactly where Hemingway was. He drove his yellow Ford sedan down to Sloppy Joe's. Charles was unable, however, to persuade Ernest to leave. He returned to the Hemingway home and told Pauline: "He's talking to a beautiful blonde in a black dress. Says he'll meet us later at Pena's."

The plan had always been to enjoy an excellent Florida lobster dinner prepared with high skill by cook Miriam Williams and then to adjourn to Pena's Garden of Roses, a Key West beer garden. Pauline was not particularly concerned, but then she hadn't seen the beautiful blonde. That happened at Pena's when Ernest introduced her to Martha Gellhorn, a novelist, a journalist, and, most dangerous of all, a beauty with long, blonde hair and long, shapely legs. Still, Pauline could not possibly have guessed that Martha would become the third Mrs. Ernest Hemingway.

Skinner, the three-hundred-pound black bartender at Sloppy Joe's, described the Martha-Ernest meeting as a meeting between "beauty and the beast." She was fetchingly attired in a black cotton sundress; he was sloppily dressed in a T-shirt and dirty Basque fishing shorts held up by a hemp rope in place of a belt. Ernest was delighted to meet a fellow novelist, particularly one who had read his books. They talked for hours.

Martha stayed on at the Colonial Hotel on Duval Street to work on a book. Soon she was invited to the Hemingway home. Said Miriam Williams: "There would be parties and Mr. Ernest and Miss Martha would be outside and kissing and carrying on, and I'd say to Miss Ada, 'Look at that, would you.' The way some people act."

Right after Martha left Key West, so did Ernest. In fact, they met in Miami and traveled together by train to New York. There he met with executives at the North American Newspaper Alliance and negotiated a contract for coverage of the Spanish Civil War. He was to be paid $500 for each cabled story, $1,000 for longer pieces that were mailed. Soon after Hemingway reached Madrid, Martha appeared, armed with a contract to cover the war for *Collier's* magazine, whose publisher Ernest had punched out in Bimini.

The affair with Martha marked the beginning of Hemingway's break with Pauline, Key West, and the country of his birth. He began to spend less time on the island. The Thompsons were still friends but a coolness had arisen. Elsewhere around town, he met disapproving glances. He no longer was the Mahatma who could do no wrong.

Even the city was changing. The vision of Julius Stone and the hurricane of '35 had conspired to create a new Key West. Stone had set about converting a bankrupt fishing village into a tourist destination, building such attractions as the Key West Aquarium and providing more accommodations and amenities for visitors. Then, after the hurricane destroyed the railroad tracks, the FEC sold its Keys' bridges and right-of-way to the federal government. By 1938, the government had completed the Overseas Highway along the former railroad tracks. US 1 now extended all the way to the southeast tip of Key West. The island was finally accessible to lower-income tourists who drove down in the family car. Ernest was not comfortable with gawking sightseers.

When he wasn't in Spain, Hemingway was spending more and more time in Havana. He put on weight, fleshing out to 215, and his

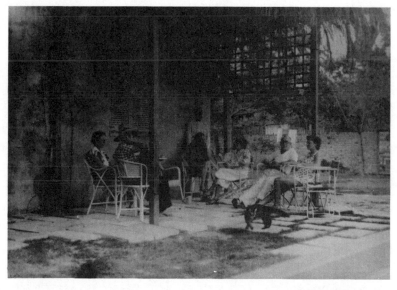

Wright and Joan Langley

After the divorce a group which doesn't include Ernest gathers at the Hemingway home. Left to right are Lorine Thompson, Ester Anderson Chambers, Jane Mason, an unidentified man in back, Pauline, James "Sully" Sullivan, and Ginny Pfeiffer, Pauline's sister.

often-terrible temper was getting the best of him all too frequently. When he couldn't find the key to his workroom, he seized a pistol and angrily shot the lock off. Pauline gave a party at the Havana Madrid night club on Front Street. Ernest spoiled it by getting into a fight, resulting in $187 in damages.

For awhile, Pauline rented an East 50th Street apartment in New York, near a private school where she had enrolled the boys. Ernest's visits to Havana became longer and more frequent. Martha leased an old estate near Havana for them. It was called La Finca Vigia, the "watchtower." Here he continued to work on his novel of the Spanish Civil War. The manuscript had swollen to some two hundred thousand words.

Martha went with him to his new U.S. hangout, Sun Valley, an Idaho ski resort. When she left in early November 1939 to go back to work in Europe, Ernest was seized with a bout of loneliness. He wanted to spend Christmas with his children and Pauline in Key West. Instead, she took the boys and flew to New York for the holidays.

On December 17, Ernest arrived at an empty house. No one was around except the gardener and his three children. Ernest stayed in the city for nine days, avoiding his old friends. He worked mornings and afternoons on *For Whom the Bell Tolls* and took his meals at downtown restaurants in a city that would not be his again until after his death.

He stayed in the empty house on Christmas Day, perhaps as a penance, James McLendon writes. On December 26, 1939, he packed his books and personal items in his Buick and boarded the ferry for Cuba. For most of the rest of his life, he would live at La Finca Vigia in the village of San Francisco de Paula. For Ernest Miller Hemingway, age forty, the toot of the Havana ferry whistle signaled farewell to Key West.

❖

CHAPTER XII

❖ ❖ ❖ ❖ ❖ ❖ ❖ ❖ ❖ ❖ ❖

PAPA LIVES

IT WAS HEMINGWAY'S TOWN when he lived here. It's still his town. His impact today is so powerful, it's hard to realize he is no longer around, walking at his jaunty pace down Duval Street, drinking a Scotch at Sloppy Joe's, tying up *Pilar* at the dock after a day of fishing in the Stream. Papa's face looks out at you from T-shirts bouncing along on the exciting anatomy of nubile young women or squeezed across the chests and potbellies of dedicated beer drinkers. You lift your Margarita and the face of the man looks up at you from the drink's coaster. There are Hemingway caps and Hemingway sweatshirts. Hemingway's House, now a museum, is the island's number one attraction, and the bar where he drank, Sloppy Joe's, is the most popular saloon in town. There are a Hemingway fishing tournament and a Hemingway Days Festival. There is even a Hemingway look-alike contest, during which Sloppy Joe's bulges with enough Papa clones to make you forget the Elvis sightings in Nashville or Las Vegas.

Hemingway left Key West at the end of December 1939. He, of course, continued to visit his American hometown for the rest of his life, usually for short stays. His old friends who had sided with Pauline in the divorce came back to him, though the friendships could never again be as close as they were in the days when a Key Wester's greatest honor was membership in the Mob.

On July 2, 1961, Ernest Hemingway killed himself in Ketchum, Idaho, shortly before his July 21st birthday. It is his birthday that is commemorated in Key West with the annual Hemingway Days Festival every summer. What is remembered is not his death but the bacchanalian joy of living of one of the twentieth century's greatest writers and one of its most entertaining legends.

HEMINGWAY DAYS

July in Key West. Hot. Steamy hot with the spell of a tropical sun baking the land below. But who cares? The streets by late afternoon are filled with noisy, happy throngs living it up in Margaritaville. Hemingway Days Festival honors the July birthday of the patron saint of the island, Papa, the Great Mother of all Big Daddies. Thousands of revelers descend upon Key West for a week-long celebration of the man as a writer (for the first part of the week) and as a zestful lover of life (for the second part, when Key West turns into a mini Mardi Gras).

Fittingly enough, the festival's birthplace was Sloppy Joe's, which was already tying Papa into its promotions. In 1981, Michael Whalton, manager of the saloon, read in the *Wall Street Journal* about a "bad Hemingway" contest in Los Angeles, a competition among parody writers. Why, he wondered, didn't Key West have an event to honor the man?

Though not officially a Conch—he was born in Miami—Whalton has strong Key West ties. He is a descendant of an old island family, which includes a famous, turn-of-the-century judge, and can even point proudly to a Whalton Street, an honor Hemingway never attained. (Ironically, Key West does have a Pauline Street, though it was named for a much earlier Pauline than Ernest's second wife.) Michael pursued the idea with Ernest's brother, Leicester. The timing fell into place—the weekend closest to Ernest's July 21st birthday, a dead time in a city that depended on tourism.

The 1981 Hemingway Days Festival emerged as a three-day event—a street fair, a "running of the bulls," a short story competition, and a Hemingway look-alike contest. Leicester volunteered to judge the short stories, ably backed up by his daughter Hilary and Lorian Hemingway, the author's granddaughter.

"We didn't know how many would show up for the look-alike contest," said Whalton. "I called everybody I knew who had a beard. Show up if you can, I told them. We had about twelve or thirteen for the first night, about the same number the next night, then about seven or eight for the finals on Saturday night. Tom Feeney was a clear-cut winner."

The only failure in the first festival was the running of the bulls, a bizarre tribute to the famous dash in Pamplona, Spain, immortalized in *The Sun Also Rises*. In the Hemingway Days variation, contestants did not attempt to outrun killer bulls but actually competed as bulls. Prizes were awarded to the best-dressed and fastest bulls. "The run was only a block long but the temperature was ninety-two, too hot for a bull costume," said Whalton. The bull event was never repeated.

The following year, the newly created Key West Tourist Development Council contributed funds and the festival began to blossom. That same year, Leicester temporarily switched the dates of his Hemingway Billfish Tournament to beef up the festival. Most important of all, the Hemingway House and Museum signed on as a sponsor. It became the site of the first "Characters in Costume" Party. Great souls stepped from the pages of his books and walked the house and grounds of his Key West mansion—Lady Brett Ashley and Jake Barnes, Santiago (the old fisherman), Nick Adams, Pilar (the woman, not the boat), Harry Morgan, and, oddly enough, a Portuguese man-of-war.

From early on, the festival was staunchly supported by Ernest's extended family: his brother, Les, until his death in 1982; Les's widow, Doris, and their daughters, screenwriter Hilary Hemingway Freundlich and Anne; Patrick's daughter, Edwina (Mina); Gregory's son, Edward, and novelist daughter, Lorian, and Lorian's daughter, Cristen. Lorian, whose novel *Walking into the River* was published in October 1982 by Simon and Schuster, coordinated the short story contest, ensuring Hemingway blood in establishing high standards.

Within three years, the festival had clearly established itself. Recalling the author's love of fisticuffs, Whalton added boxing exhibitions at a ring set up in the yard at the Hemingway House. One year, two of Ernest's old sparring partners participated. Iron Baby Roberts refereed and Shine Forbes served as a judge. Songwriter

Hemingway Days Festival

A group of Hemingway Days revelers includes Look-Alike winners and Hemingway family members; back row, left to right: Bill Young, Hollywood, Florida; Leo Rost, Boynton Beach; Michael Dallett, Fort Lauderdale; and Nick Parrish, Pompano Beach; front row: Cristen Hemingway Jaynes, Ernest's great granddaughter; her mother, Lorian Hemingway; and Hilary Hemingway Freundlich, daughter of Leicester Hemingway.

Jimmy Buffett, who would later succumb to the Key West spell and become a novelist himself, volunteered to sing the national anthem before the matches. When a commemorative Ernest Hemingway stamp was issued by the U.S. Postal Service, it was unveiled in Key West as part of the 1989 Hemingway Days Festival. The stamp featured the memorable 1957 photograph by Gerald Karsh, the same picture that adorns Sloppy Joe's T-shirts.

By the mid-1980s, droves of beefy, bearded Papa clones were roaming Duval Street, looking for a drink to psych themselves up for the fierce competition. Some bring cheering sections; others print up posters and flyers drumming up support. The look-alike contest has become far and away the most popular event of the festival, so popular in fact that even Oak Park, the sedate Midwestern city where Ernest was born, now holds one of its own. The Key West version attracts entrants from all over the country and from Europe; the 1991 winner was from Santa Fe. By 1992, the number of look-alikes had risen to eighty-three, one from as far away as Hawaii.

One of the entrants, Norman Levin, from nearby Fort Lauderdale, brought a marital touch to the contest, perhaps an indirect tribute to Hemingway, who, like Levin, married four times. Norman had entered the contest every year since 1985 without winning. In 1992, he fell short again but won something more important—the hand of his bride. The wedding invitation announced the nuptials of Norman "Papa" Levin and Paula "Pauline" Shapiro of Baltimore. The wedding was held just prior to the contest. Music was non-traditional. As they marched down an aisle of look-alikes, a Frank Sinatra record delivered the strains of "Young at Heart." After the ceremony, exit music was the island anthem, Jimmy Buffett's immortal "Why Don't We Get Drunk and Screw." Only in Key West, as Papa would have said.

Like Levin, many of the look-alikes enter the contest year after year. George Burley, fifty-seven, of Tierra Verde, Florida, near St. Petersburg, won in 1992 after four unsuccessful tries. "Maybe it's because I'm older and the beard's a little grayer," he said. "I feel more like him than ever before."

The 1992 festival, which drew close to ten thousand people, included a wide variety of events, some of which would have delighted Papa, some of which would probably have infuriated him. After all, he did loath tourism and its inevitable end-product, tourists. Key West radio featured a Hemingway trivia contest, and a storytelling contest was held at the Ocean Key House. Guided walking tours in the early evening acquainted visitors with the city's rich literary heritage for which Hemingway could claim considerable credit. On Friday night, the Hemingway House and Museum hosted a party with music. For the athletic, the festival offered back-country kayak tours, a golf tournament, sailing races, the annual arm-wrestling contest, and a 5K sunset run, which drew a winner from Norway. Another contestant, Dave Meeker, was from Sacramento, California. His devotion to Hemingway runs so deep that his book store is named Nick Adams and Company, Rare Books.

As the fiesta developed, its founding fathers realized the festival had overemphasized one Hemingway at the expense of the other. During his highly public life, he had emerged as two people—one a swaggering macho figure, the other a disciplined artist of rare genius. In the alcoholic haze of Hemingway Days, the writer had been shunted over to a table in the corner of a noisy barroom. In 1986, the festival's founders moved to correct the problem.

In 1987, Dr. James Plath, assistant professor of English at Illinois Wesleyan University, was planning a Hemingway/Key West edition of *The Clockwatch Review*, a "little" magazine he edits and publishes. For the special edition, he asked Lorian Hemingway, whose stories had appeared in such varied publications as *Rolling Stone, Penthouse*, and *The New York Times Sunday Magazine*, to write an article on her great-uncle, Leicester Hemingway. When Lorian learned that Plath would be visiting Key West at Hemingway Days to interview Jimmy Buffett for the review, she asked him to serve as a judge for the short story contest.

Hemingway Days Festival

Principals in the Hemingway Days Writers Workshop and Conference include author and Hemingway scholar Dr. James Nagel; screenwriter Hilary Hemingway Freundlich; Dr. James Plath, Workshop director; and novelist Lorian Hemingway.

From this Key West meeting between Lorian and Plath grew the Hemingway Days Writer's Workshop and Conference. "The impetus," Lorian said, "was the success of the annual Key West Literary Seminar." The first workshop, held in 1988, drew just twelve registrants. By 1992, it had grown into a three-day session, featuring well-known writers, including James Dickey, author of *Deliverance* and winner of the National Book Award for *Buckdancer's Choice.* Dickey was further honored with the first Conch Republic Prize for Literature. Others on the workshop staff were James W. Hall, author of three novels set in the Keys—*Bones of Coral, Under Cover of Daylight,* and *Tropical Freeze*—and James Nagel, professor of English at the University of Georgia, Hemingway scholar, and author of *Hemingway in Love and War.*

"The idea of the workshops was to add a serious dimension to the festival," said Plath, who appeared at a Friday night party at the Hemingway House clad in the Pamplona bull runner's classic white togs, accented with red sash. Less than two weeks earlier, he had run ahead of the bulls in Spain. "We wanted to give people something of

91

substance to take back, something more than T-shirts."

Plath is attracted to Key West by many of the same elements that appealed to Hemingway. "The air is dense, rich, thick, strikes you in the face," he said. "Key West is a visual potpourri, plants fifty feet tall, tropical flora and fauna. Many of the elements that drew Hemingway are still in place, the sea, the fishing. And a dynamic, robust lifestyle. That's the Key West personality."

Plath, an authority on the relationship between modern art and the work of Hemingway, compares the author in one sense to the famous Spanish surrealist Salvador Dali: "They were the first successful promoters in their respective art forms." That sense of self-promotion played a major role in creating the author's 1990's image. Said Plath: "Hemingway was raised on romantic legends. He understood their power. Now Hemingway cults have grown up. He's been set up as a guru, a figure who represents escapism, romance. He's also a symbol of what people would like to do with their lives. Today it's the Hemingway legend that is celebrated."

The "legend" may have been part of the problem that curtailed Hemingway Days. Friction among festival promoters, the look-alikes, and the Hemingway family led to the end of the festival in 1997 as it was originally conceived. Part of the tribute to the old master continues, however, in the eternally popular Look-Alike Contest.

Key West's biggest Hemingway literary event was the third annual Key West Literary Seminar, held in January 1985 at the Tennessee Williams Fine Arts Center. The entire three-day program was devoted to Papa. Digby Diehl, book editor of the *Los Angeles Examiner,* summed it up well: "During three days of intensive study, experts described how Hemingway fished for marlin, drank rum, sparred with his pals, and wrote six of his greatest works here. And his spirit is still alive in the old haunts, they implied. You need only the courage—and the liver—to search, bar after bar, for Papa."

Among the Hemingway authorities who spoke at the seminar were George Plimpton, founder and editor of the *Paris Review;*

Charles Scribner Jr., representing Hemingway's publisher; Papa's son, Patrick, returning to his childhood home for the first time in nearly thirty-five years; and a number of Hemingway scholars and authors, among them Bernice Kert, Robert Gajdusik, James Nagel, Scott Donaldson, David Kaufelt, Linda Wagner, Paul Smith, Allen Josephs, Frank Laurance, and Tim O'Brien. Playwright John DeGroot's one-man play, *Papa*, had its world premiere as a workshop performance.

Papa, the legend, has a greater impact on Key West today than Hemingway, the writer, had when he lived here. He was the town's celebrity then but the glow faded after he moved to Cuba. Joan Langley, a Conch, who with her late husband, Wright, operated the publishing company Langley Press, recalls growing up in Key West: "In high school we read Tennessee Williams, not Hemingway. I never read him until I went away to Duke. Our neighbor was Charles Thompson, and my father worked for Norberg Thompson. I never dreamed that Mr. Sullivan, a very nice old man, had been a drinking buddy of Hemingway's. He used to repair my tricycle. We used to hear stories that Hemingway's mob would go to Sully's machine shop to sniff oxygen to cure their hangovers."

The late Wright Langley, author of three books on the Keys, one in collaboration with wife Joan, called Hemingway "a fairly recent phenomenon." Langley was a historical consultant who specialized in Key West and the Florida Keys following fifteen years as manager of the Historical Florida Keys Preservation Board. Langley Press published a 1990 edition of *Papa*, James McLendon's book on Hemingway's Key West years. A native of North Carolina, Langley arrived in Key West in 1965 to work as a reporter for the *Miami Herald*'s Keys Bureau.

"In nineteen sixty-five, not that much attention was paid to Hemingway. You might drop by Hemingway's bar, Sloppy Joe's, in late afternoon and find maybe ten people in there." Tourism began to bloom, he believed, after the 1976 Bicentennial, when a strong program of restoration coupled with more promotion began the upswing. Meanwhile, both the Hemingway House and Museum and Sloppy Joe's increased their promotion, thus setting the stage for Hemingway Days and the formation of the Tourist Development Commission in the early 1980s. Media coverage has been steady for both the Hemingway House and Sloppy Joe's. On a November morning, Sloppy Joe's manager John Klausing was interviewed for the syndicated television show *A Current Affair* one day after being invaded by group of eleven Dutch reporters.

Most active in exploiting Hemingway has been Sloppy Joe's. The heavy promotion began in the late 1970s, when Stan Smith began selling T-shirts featuring the famous Gerald Karsh photograph of the author in his later years. Sightings of these shirts have been reported from Europe, Africa, and Australia. Sloppy Joe's sells one hundred thousand of the shirts every year, says manager Klausing. The saloon also sells Hemingway polo shirts, muscle

Photo by Stuart McIver

Key West's 1990s *Pilar*, a charterboat and floating Hemingway Museum.

shirts, sweatshirts, ponchos, caps and straw hats, coasters, mugs, shot glasses, pens, and postcards. For $4.25, you can try one of Hemingway's favorite drinks, the Papa Dobles, a Daiquiri variation that uses ruby red grapefruit, cherry juice, and rum.

Sloppy Joe's also functions as a Hemingway museum. Its walls are covered with photographs of the man and his worldwide activities. Erik Smith's 1933 WPA-period painting showing Hemingway at work still hangs in the bar, as does a contemporary painting of Sloppy Joe's by Carol Sadowski of Hollywood, Florida. Actually the town is home to three Hemingway museums: the Hemingway House, the largest and most popular; Sloppy Joe's, where the drinks rank somewhat higher than the memorabilia; and a small one aboard Tex Phillips' *Pilar II*. Built in the 1930s to roughly the same specifications as Papa's boat, the Phillips craft houses a collection of photographs, a watercolor, and movie posters from films made from Hemingway's books.

Novelist David Kaufelt, who conducts walking tours of the island's literary sites, wrote in *The Book Lover's Guide to Florida*: "Hemingway, America's first great literary media celebrity, an early master of publicity spin, came via Cuba from Europe on the recommendation of his friend, John Dos Passos, who had visited during a walking tour. Hemingway arrived at the beginning of his fame and the onset of his personal myth. His life in Key West was well chronicled in Pathe newsreels and *Life* magazine, helping to create an image of Key West as a writers' haven."

Long after Hemingway left Key West for Cuba, his aura continued to pull novelists, playwrights, poets, biographers, historians, editors, and publishers into his magnetic field. In *Key West Writers and Their Houses*, Lynn Mitsuko Kaufelt, David's wife, wrote: "I believe the reason so many writers thrive in Key West is that the houses they write in and the houses around them are filled with the traditions and the histories and the life that helped spark that elusive creative fire." The Key West literary colony has included poets Elizabeth Bishop,

Richard Wilbur, James Merrill, and John Malcolm Brinnan; novelists Phil Caputo, Robert Stone, Thomas Sanchez, and Thomas McGuane; and America's premier playwright, Tennessee Williams.

"I feel that Hemingway's spirit remains in the sea, contained in a fabled big marlin forever circling our island, threatening and challenging and ultimately encouraging those following in his wake," explained David Kaufelt. "Key West suddenly became this literary place, mostly because of Hemingway."

Painters feel the pull of Papa too. Artist Carol Sadowski, compared by one art critic with the American painter Edward Hopper, visited the Hemingway House for the first time in 1977. Since then she has gone on to paint nearly forty pictures interpreting Hemingway themes, starting with Key West and then branching out to his other locales: Paris, Spain, Bimini, Cuba, and Oak Park, Illinois.

Obviously a presence as mighty as Ernest Hemingway's does not go quietly into the tropical night. Traces of his Key West days mingle everywhere with commercial tie-ins. Authors and scholars search the town, looking for Hemingway, the writer. Others inhale his legend through a tour of his house, a day in the Gulf Stream stalking the mighty marlin, or a night of pub-crawling in the saloons of Key West.

It really doesn't matter where you go. He's still here.

LOOK-ALIKES

Hemingways to the right of me. Hemingways to the left of me. Too many Hemingways. Eighty-three altogether—and I was one of those Papa clones, packed like olives in the sweltering heat of Sloppy Joe's.

Each July, Key West lures tourists to the Conch Republic with its annual Hemingway Days Festival, timed to honor the birthday of the city's favorite son. The most popular event: the Hemingway look-alike contest.

Thirty-five of us Papas were clustered around the stage, gazing

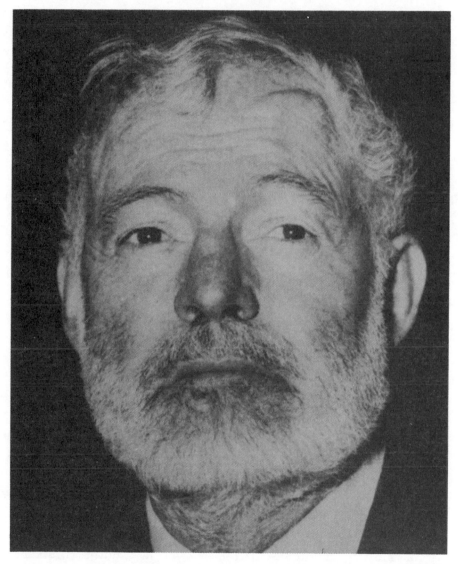

Sloppy Joe's

The Look-Alike contest aims at the appearance of the Great Man sported in the late 1950s, as in this 1959 photograph, taken in Pamplona, Spain.

97

out at a sweating, beer- and/or tequila-guzzling multitude that had overwhelmed Hemingway's favorite saloon. Overhead, paddle fans swirled the hot, beery vapors and the deafening sounds of a country rock band. Any minute now, I would be going out onstage to do my best to look, swagger, and sound like the Great Man. In my head, I rehearsed my lines again and waited. And waited. Ruth Chados, contest coordinator, told me: "Keep it short. Tell them it's time to party. They've been drinking for hours and they're in no mood to hear a speech."

On the drive down from Broward County, I had rehearsed my lines. I would dazzle the crowd and the judges—former winners and members of the Hemingway family—with a great Hemingway quote, backed up with an impressive stage prop. I would swagger out with a half-empty bottle of champagne in my hand, and, in spellbinding fashion, I would deliver one of my favorite Hemingway quotes: "The half empty champagne bottle is the enemy of mankind."

I would move then to Phase 2, the literary element, a high-toned touch I was sure no one else would duplicate. I would deliver the earth-shaking announcement that I was writing a book on Papa. This had to be a winner with judges and crowd.

"We seek the older, heavier-set Hemingway look-alike with the full beard. Judging is based on the personal appearance," read the guidelines. Hefty, burly, bearded. I decided to wear khaki shorts and a khaki shirt, enhanced by a touch of Hemingway realism. Papa often held his khaki shorts up not by a belt but by a piece of rope that sometimes smelled of dead fish. I skipped the dead-fish touch. I donned my khaki outfit, tied a rope around my middle, combed my hair and beard, then sprayed them with hair glue.

Why did I think I might win this contest? I wasn't nearly hefty enough. I'm just six feet tall and weigh about 180. He was six two and weighed about 220, sometimes even more. His face was round, mine long and thin. But then I had a secret weapon. I looked like other people. Something about my face tapped into a giant Everyman mother lode. Most of my look-alike experiences were harmless, but a couple bordered on dangerous.

Years ago, for example, as a young sportswriter for a North Carolina daily, I covered a fight between a local favorite, Mickey Whelan, and a visiting welterweight, one Irish Johnny Taylor. The fight ended early. Irish Johnny hit Mickey below the belt and Mickey couldn't go on. Fight fans were not happy. After the fight, the crowd mistook me for Irish Johnny. I had to run to get away from a howling mob.

Then in Washington, at Ebbitt's Old Ale House, a historic saloon that claimed Abe Lincoln as a satisfied customer, a mean-looking character with an eye twitch said to me, "You think we aren't on to you. You FBI people think you can get away with anything. You haven't got anything on us and you're not going to." His eye kept twitching and I felt like mine would start up soon. I left.

My uncle Bob was a friend of the family of the great North Carolina novelist Thomas Wolfe, a contemporary of Hemingway's. One night he took me to one of the Washington suburbs to visit Wolfe's sister, Mabel, better known as Helen Gant in Wolfe's most famous novel, *Look Homeward, Angel*. As we sat on her front porch one summer night, she said, "Mr. McIver, how strange. The way the light hits you, you look like Tom."

Another time I got on an elevator in a Baltimore hotel with powerful U.S. Senator Millard Tydings. "Young man," he said, "you remind me of an actor I used to know, Frank Craven." I was flattered. Craven had starred in Thornton Wilder's *Our Town* on Broadway, not to mention assorted movies.

You can see why I thought I might have a shot at winning the Hemingway contest. All I needed was a judging panel of Senator Tydings, Mabel Wolfe Wheaton, and an angry mob of fight fans. When I got to Sloppy Joe's, I told Ruth Chados, "I've got two speeches: one thirty seconds, one sixty seconds."

She stared at me in wonderment. "You've got about twenty seconds; fifteen would be better. These people have been drinking for hours. They have no attention span."

Mike Whalton, festival director, announced the prizes, among them a week for two at the Ocean Key House, a $100 bar tab at Sloppy Joe's, and "last of all, an oil change at Boa's Tire and Auto Service." The oil change got a laugh.

Next he began to call up Hemingways in groups of five. I watched with dismay. All were burlier than I was and clearly rounder of face. And their messages to the throng were all brief, mostly calls to the faithful to drink up. Some clones had their own cheering sections. Many had competed in the contest for years. One, the aptly named George Burley, said it was his fifth try.

I stood just offstage, my half-empty champagne bottle resting on the table of a happy band of revelers. Then I heard my name

Photo by Peter Colelli
The author with a beard grown for the Hemingway Look-Alike Contest.

called. I just left the champagne bottle there. Later some waitress would pick it up and be completely mystified. A half-empty champagne bottle in a beer and tequila room. And to make it even more mysterious, the bottle was in a J.C. Penney bag.

Waves of heat and room noise buffeted me. I tried to swagger as I said, "One true sentence, as Hemingway would put it." I felt a brief wave of disapproval. Was I going to be one of those talkers? I went on with the true sentence: "The best place in the world to be today is Sloppy Joe's." Mild approval. I decided to take a chance. "One more true sentence: my car does need an oil change." Finally, a ripple of subdued laughter. The only laughter to gladden my heart was that of Hilary Hemingway Freundlich, Ernest's niece, who just happened to be one of the judges. Maybe I might get Hilary's vote.

Thirty-five Hemingways were trotted up onstage that night. Nine qualified for the Saturday night finals. Somehow my name didn't get called. Five months later, I met Lorian Hemingway, Ernest's granddaughter. She advised: "If you're going to enter the contest again, gain some weight—a lot of weight."

In the Saturday night finals, George Burley won on his fifth try and I was left to ponder why I didn't win. The main reason, I think, was that there were at least a dozen people there who looked more like Hemingway than I did—heftier, rounder of face, earthier. But there was something else. I think I impersonated the wrong Hemingway.

Two Hemingways left their mark on this world. One was a dedicated, disciplined writer, winner of the Nobel Prize, one of the two or three most important writers of the twentieth century. The other was a self-promoting celebrity who projected to the world the image of Papa, a man who could shoot more big game, catch bigger sailfish, get into more fights, chase more women, and drink more booze than anybody else on the planet. That Hemingway was the quintessential party animal, the patron saint of Key West. He is the Hemingway who is honored at Sloppy Joe's every July—a lover of life, joyful and exuberant. The men all wanted to be like him, the women all wanted to spend the night with him.

Party on, Papa.

CONCH REPUBLIC

In the spring of 1982, the Reagan Administration set up a roadblock just south of Florida City on US 1, the only road to Key West. On a Sunday afternoon, the United States Border Patrol began stopping all cars coming back to the mainland from the Keys. Weary, sunburned tourists were checked for illegal drugs and aliens. Traffic backed up for twenty-three miles. Tempers and bladders backed up for at least as far.

Irate motorists protested, and attorneys challenged the clumsy, ineffective blockade in the courts. The Conchs, of course, were livid. The Keys depended on tourism, and the government was harassing credit card–carrying, money-spending tourists. There was only one answer: war.

The idea for the Conch Republic was born on April 20, 1982. Key West Mayor Dennis Wardlow and five other revolutionaries— Dennis Bitner, William E. Smith, Edwin O. Swift III, Townsend Keiffer, and John Magiola—met to plot a counterstrike. Three days later, the six "Conch Reveres" called a town meeting at noon in Mallory Square, named after a Key West Confederate hero who had seceded more than a century earlier.

Their call that April day was for Key West to secede from the Union, form the Conch Republic, and declare war on the tyrant. A Conch Republic flag was raised on high. Impassioned speeches were made, a few ambassadorships were passed out, and a loaf of stale Cuban bread was tossed aloft to symbolize, somewhat murkily, a declaration of war against the United States.

Then, suddenly, the Conch Republic surrendered and applied for foreign aid. The aid was fast in coming. The roadblock was lifted. The party lasted a week. Since then Conch Republic Days has become an annual event. Border passes and passports are printed and silver coins, T-shirts, and flags are sold. The Conch Republic, born from an assault on tourism, quickly became another sterling idea for promoting Key West tourism. Wardlow continues as prime minister.

The Hemingway boys, Ernest and Les, got there first with the idea even though Ernest was dead set against tourists taking over his island. Still, here's what he said in a revolutionary letter written to John Dos Passos from Key West on April 12, 1932, almost exactly fifty years before the Conch Republic was born. He proposed that Key West secede from the Union immediately, the day after the Navy and Marines began to deactivate the naval base. He called for the establishment of the South Western Island Republic, which he referred to as the Most Prosperous Island in the World, the Paris of the South West, a free and decidedly free-wheeling port featuring a gigantic liquor warehouse. He proposed blowing up the Bahia Honda Viaduct, burning bridges, and destroying all buoys and light-houses.

Ernest had some bloody plans and an approach guaranteed to offend everyone. Among other things, he planned to re-enslave the blacks and use the car ferries to smuggle in "chinamen." Decidedly not politically correct.

On the first three nights, he called for the massacre of the Catholics, Jews, Protestants, free thinkers, atheists, Communists, and members of the lighthouse service, in that order. He suggested knocking off a few counterrevolutionaries and then burning the town after a day of fishing. The fifth and sixth days would be free for "members of the party" to do as they liked. "On the seventh day," he wrote, "we elect Butstein (Dos Passos' wife, Katy) the Goddess of Reason and order MacLeish to write an Epic Poem about the Movement. Late that evening we shoot MacLeish as his poem has turned out Lousy and send for Evan Shipman (another poet friend of Hemingway's). You can see how it will be. Just one gay hilarious round with everyone busy and happy. At the end of twelve days we raise wages to beat hell and massacre the poles."

Leicester, on the other hand, had a plan that was much more elaborate and not at all bloody. His republic was not located at Key West. New Atlantis, as he called his island nation, was a raft anchored off the south coast of Jamaica in the early 1960s. Lorian Hemingway, Ernest's granddaughter, wrote a funny account of New Atlantis in *The Clockwatch Review* in 1986: "The flag for New Atlantis was stitched by Les's wife, Doris. It was made of dark blue cloth, with a white interior triangle representing the Bermuda Triangle. The white piece of cloth was salvaged from one of Hilary's diapers. Les and a friend took a hollowed-out log canoe to the site of New Atlantis, which had been raised on a sea mount, to raise the new country's flag. Les hoped to receive mail on the raft in time. He processed stamps for the new country, and minted coins. He was president then of a country wrought from idealism and a sense of humor. The Constitution of New Atlantis was modeled after that of the United States. . . . The truth is that Les Hemingway could have stood in shallow water and proclaimed himself an island and republic unto himself."

❖

CHAPTER XIII

❖ ❖ ❖ ❖ ❖ ❖ ❖ ❖ ❖ ❖ ❖

WALK WITH PAPA
A WALKING TOUR OF KEY WEST

EVERYWHERE YOU GO ON THE ISLAND, his face looks out at you, mostly from T-shirts, sometimes from coasters underneath a drink, sometimes from posters advertising Hemingway Days or literary seminars. Burly men who may never have read any of his books or stories grow beards in the heat of a Key West July to compete in Hemingway look-alike contests.

No doubt about it—Ernest "Papa" Hemingway is the favorite son of Key West, the human logo of the exotic, hedonistic island that lies at the tip of the Florida Keys, an island he called "the St. Tropez of the poor." Here for over a decade, he lived, fathered children, made friends and enemies, ate, drank, fished, fought, created his macho image, chased after women, worshipped, ripped his second marriage apart, and somewhere along the way found time to write all or part of five fiction and nonfiction books; a play, *The Fifth Column*; and two of his most famous short stories, "The Snows of Kilimanjaro" and "The Short Happy Life of Francis Macomber."

The Great Man left his stamp on Key West. It was his town then. It's his town now. Let's trace a few of his large footsteps with a self-guided tour of Hemingway's hangouts, most of them in the north-western part of the island, an area called Old Town. The starting place has to be his home at 907 Whitehead Street. Allow yourself forty-five minutes for the tour of his home. The walk, which is roughly two miles long, should take you between one and a half and two hours.

HEMINGWAY HOUSE

After the many cold winters he spent in tiny Paris apartments, the spacious, lushly landscaped Spanish Colonial mansion built in 1851 of coral rock brought to Hemingway the spell of the tropics. In December 1931, Ernest and his second wife, Pauline Pfeiffer, moved into their new home, a wedding present from Pauline's wealthy uncle, Gus Pfeiffer. It cost Uncle Gus just $8,000 then.

A restless expatriate who lived most of his adult life outside his

Historical Association of Southern Florida

The Hemingway House, the start of the Hemingway Walking Tour.

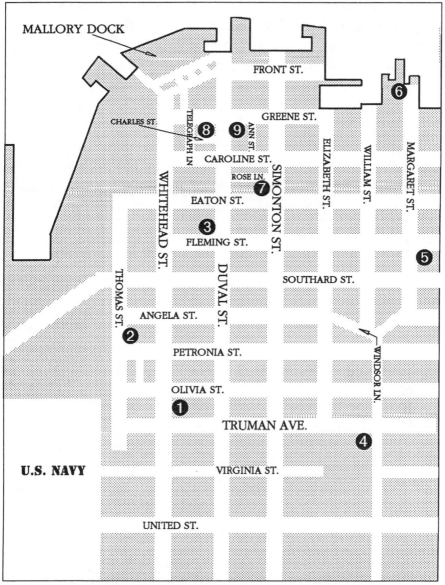

HEMINGWAY WALKING TOUR

1. Hemingway House
2. Boxing Arena
3. Colonial Hotel
4. St. Mary
5. Electric Kitchen
6. Thompson's Docks
7. First Apartment
8. First Sloppy Joe's
9. Second Sloppy Joe's

native land, Hemingway seemed most at home in his own country in Depression-era Key West. Certainly, it was in this house that he worked best. Seated in a Cuban cigarmaker's wooden chair, the author went to work early and wrote in longhand in an open room uncluttered with furniture on the second floor of the former carriage house. A good morning's work, he said, was "seven pencils." Bookshelves and trophies from his big game hunting expeditions still adorn the walls. The first room remodeled after the Hemingways moved in, the studio was entered via a second-story catwalk from the house. Today visitors on guided tours of the house climb outside stairs to see where the author worked.

While Ernest was in Spain in 1937, Pauline had a swimming pool built as a surprise for her roving husband. The first ever built in Key West, it cost $20,000, two and a half times the purchase price of the house. His reaction was unexpected. Reaching into his pocket, he pulled out a penny and threw it to the ground, angrily accusing Pauline of spending his last cent on the pool. Actually, it was her money. She took it all in good humor. She retrieved the penny and had it cemented into the ground with a glass covering. Visitors get a good laugh at Papa's last penny.

The grounds swarm with beautiful, six-toed cats. One legend has it that Ernest acquired a urinal from Sloppy Joe's, put it on his back and carried it to his home to serve as a watering trough for his cats.

After the death of Hemingway in 1961, the house was sold to Mrs. Bernice Dickson. A Registered National Historic Landmark, the Hemingway House is open every day from 9:00 A.M. to 5:00 P.M. for guided tours. A gift shop sells T-shirts, note cards, pictures, and books by and about Hemingway.

Next, walk north on Whitehead, turn left at Petronia Street, then proceed for two blocks to the northeast corner of the intersection with Thomas Street.

Photo by Stuart McIver

Where fists once flew the Blue Heaven Pool Room and Restaurant now operate.

FISTICUFFS

Now the Blue Heaven Restaurant, in Hemingway's day this site was an open-air boxing arena where he refereed the popular Friday night fights. Many of the fighters, among them "Iron Baby" Roberts, Kermit "The Battling Geech" Forbes, and Alfred "Black Pie" Colebrooks, also boxed with Ernest in a ring in his backyard. They were paid fifty cents a round.

From the Blue Heaven Restaurant, walk back east on Petronia to Duval Street, then turn left to the northwest corner of Duval and Fleming.

COLONIAL HOTEL

In April 1928, Ernest and Pauline Hemingway visited the city for the first time, sailing into Key West from Havana aboard a Peninsular & Occidental steamship. As they approached the island, the first sight

109

Photo by Joan McIver
The Holiday Inn - La Concha Resort does business today in the "skyscraper" that gave Hemingway his first glimpse of downtown Key West.

they saw was the town's tallest building, the seven-story Key West Colonial Hotel. Later they would book visiting friends and relatives into the Colonial. Rates were reasonable: $1 to $6 a day, depending on whether you picked the American or European Plan. The hotel is still in business today as the Holiday Inn/La Concha Resort.

From La Concha, walk east on Fleming Street. At 513 Fleming, you will find the Key West Island Book Store, well stocked with books by and about Papa Hemingway. In Hemingway's time, the city's principal bookstore, owned by Leonte Valladares, was located at 517 Fleming Street. L. Valladares & Son is now at 1200 Duval Street.

Proceed to Elizabeth Street, then turn right at the Monroe County Library to Windsor Lane, then left to the Catholic church.

ST. MARY, STAR OF THE SEA

A Congregationalist in his earlier years, Hemingway converted to Catholicism when he married the devoutly Catholic Pauline. Hemingway was generous to St. Mary, Star of the Sea, recalls Betty Bruce, whose late husband, Toby, worked for Hemingway. "Ernest gave an altar to the church," she recalls.

From St. Mary, walk southwest on Windsor Lane to Passover Lane, then turn left to the Key West Cemetery. There are no Hemingway associations here, except the graves of a few of his

Photo by Joan McIver

Ernest attended Mass at St. Mary, Star of the Sea.

friends, but you might want to look at the monument to the sailors killed in the explosion of the USS *Maine* in 1898 or, if you can find it, the headstone that proclaims, "I Told You I Was Sick."

From the cemetery, walk west on Margaret Street to the southeast corner of Margaret and Fleming Streets. Through this part of town, you are seeing the old Key West that Hemingway knew.

ELECTRIC KITCHEN

At 830 Fleming Street, Mrs. Rhoda Baker, better known as "Rutabaga," operated Mrs. Baker's Electric Kitchen. Despite the high-tech name, it was generally agreed that the only thing electric about the place was its lighting, supplied rather mundanely by a few bare light bulbs hanging from the ceiling. No matter. The food was good, plentiful, and cheap. In 1935, the Electric Kitchen offered "club breakfast, 20 cents to 45 cents; luncheon and dinner, 30 to 50 cents." Mrs. Baker's place became a favorite hangout for Hemingway's

Photo by Stuart McIver
You can no longer get a twenty-cent breakfast at 830 Fleming Street, former home of the Electric Kitchen.

Mob, a strange combination of local pals and out-of-town talent.

From the Electric Kitchen, continue north on Margaret Street to the waterfront area, now known as Land's End Village.

THOMPSON'S DOCKS

On Key West Bight, Hemingway often visited docks owned by his closest friend, Charles Thompson. The three Thompson brothers, comprising the most affluent family on the island, owned a ship's chandlery, an icehouse, a cigar box factory, a hardware and tackle store, a green turtle cannery, and large waterfront pens called the Turtle Kraals. At one time, the Thompsons controlled the green sea turtle industry in the Florida Keys and in Central America. The site of their turtle cannery is known today as Turtle Kraals, a restaurant, bar, and museum.

When he first came to Key West, Ernest, an enthusiastic fisherman since his boyhood days, had to fish from charter boats or from

Photo by Stuart McIver
Thompson's Docks would later become the Land's End Village.

the boats of his favorite Key West fishing buddies, Thompson, Sloppy Joe Russell, and Captain Bra Saunders, a Bahamian. In 1934, Hemingway had a thirty-eight-foot powerboat custom built for him at the Wheeler Shipyard in New York. He would name his boat *Pilar*. He berthed his boat not at Thompson's Docks but in the Navy Yard near the submarine pens, an area not open to the public. *Pilar* is now at Cojimar, Cuba.

From Land's End Village, go south one block to Caroline Street, then walk west to the southwest corner of Caroline and Simonton Streets.

HEMINGWAY'S FIRST KEY WEST HOME

At 314 Simonton Street stands Casa Antigua, now a large private home with shops on the first floor. Through a bizarre sequence of events, it turned out to be the first Key West domicile for the Hemingways. Pauline's uncle, Gus Pfeiffer, the principal owner of Richard Hudnut Pharmaceuticals, gave his favorite niece and her

Photo by Joan McIver

Casa Antigua, where the Hemingways stayed on their first visit to Key West, now contains shops on its first floor, among them the Pelican Poop Shoppe.

husband a superb wedding present, a yellow Model A Ford run-about. It was supposed to be waiting for them when they steamed into Key West from Havana. Unfortunately, problems with the ferry service from Miami to Key West had delayed the shipment of their new automobile.

Unable to find the car at the docks, Ernest called the local Ford dealership, the Trevor and Morris Company. Mortified that his car had not yet arrived, the dealers insisted that the Hemingways move into the Trevor and Morris Apartments, now Casa Antigua, while the problem was being worked out. The apartment, a drab set of rooms above the garage, was hardly first-rate. Its fame rests solely on its status as Ernest Hemingway's first Key West home, where he immediately resumed work on *A Farewell to Arms*.

Now turn north to Greene Street and walk west past Duval.

THE BLIND PIG/CAPTAIN TONY'S

With the end of Prohibition in 1933, Hemingway's pal Josie Russell,

Photo by Joan McIver
Known once as the Blind Pig, then Sloppy Joe's, this Greene Street institution now goes by the name of Captain Tony's.

115

charter boat captain and rumrunner, leased a dark, cavernous speakeasy at 428 Greene Street. His plan was to convert it into a legal bar. Hemingway, who somewhere along the way became Russell's silent partner, convinced Josie that "Sloppy Joe's" would be a better name for the bar than the one it already sported—the Blind Pig, a generic Florida term for a bar operating outside the law.

Since there were no closing hours in Key West, Sloppy Joe's had no doors. A rowdy fisherman's bar, it quickly became Hemingway's favorite hangout. There he met Martha Gellhorn, author and foreign correspondent, stylishly clad in a black dress and sporting an impressive mane of tawny blonde hair and a shapely pair of legs. She later became his third wife.

On May 5, 1937, Josie Russell moved Sloppy Joe's half a block to the east. The bar where Ernest met Martha continued as a Key West institution under the name Captain Tony's. Follow Sloppy Joe's move by walking east on Greene Street to the southeast corner of Greene and Duval.

SLOPPY JOE'S

When the Hemingways first arrived in Key West, the building at the southeast corner of Duval and Greene Streets housed the finest restaurant in town, the Victoria. It was owned and operated by a Spaniard with the embarrassing name of Farto. It became Sloppy Joe's because the rent at 428 Greene Street had been raised a dollar a week. Rather than pay the increased rent, Joe Russell bought the Victoria for $2,500 and moved in promptly in May 1937.

Along with the Hemingway House, Sloppy Joe's remains to this day the Key West landmark most closely identified with the literary giant—not with his literature but with his drinking and carousing. Since his death in 1961, Hemingway has become more popular than ever in Key West. Some estimates claim that a million tourists a year come into the bar to have a drink or just a peek at the Hemingway

Photo by Joan McIver
Hemingway aficionados made a point of hoisting a cold one at Sloppy Joe's.

memorabilia. Newspaper clippings adorn the walls, along with paintings by WPA-period artist Erik Smith, whose oil shows Papa, Josie, and the giant bartender, Skinner, and by contemporary painter Carol Sadowski, who depicted Sloppy Joe's in the early 1980s.

Sales of Sloppy Joe's T-shirts, featuring a likeness of Hemingway, exceed a hundred thousand a year. They are now seen around the world. Although beer is still popular, today's patrons also drink vodka, tequila and various sweet frozen drinks. Some of them even honor the master by ordering Papa Dobles, the drink created in Cuba to honor the author.

A SIDE TRIP

The Casa Marina (today known as Marriott's Casa Marina), the island's luxury hotel in Hemingway's time, is too far from other sites to fit into the walking tour. You might, however, want to drive to the hotel at 1500 Reynolds Street on the Atlantic side of Key West. It was built in 1921 by the Flagler System, the same organization that brought the railroad to Key West nine years earlier.

Photo by Joan McIver
In Hemingway's day the Casa Marina was the island's ritziest hotel.

Hemingway used to eat at the Casa Marina on occasion, usually when business acquaintances or visiting friends invited him over. The management was not happy with his disdain for their dining dress code, particularly the absence of socks on his sandaled feet. He did, however, yield slightly by wearing long trousers, hopefully with a leather belt instead of a rope.

❖

CHAPTER XIV

❖ ❖ ❖ ❖ ❖ ❖ ❖ ❖ ❖ ❖ ❖

BIMINI

EVIL SPIRITS WITH A CERTAIN SENSE OF HUMOR must have hovered over the Gulf Stream as Ernest Hemingway set forth to fish the waters of Bimini. How else could a man as gifted as Hemingway shoot at a shark and wind up hitting himself in both legs with one bullet?

In the waters near Key West, Hemingway had discovered the joys of big game fishing. He fished the Florida Keys and the Dry Tortugas and then the Gulf Stream off the north side of Cuba. And all the while he kept hearing stories of huge tuna near Bimini, the Bahamian island that called itself "the big game fishing capital of the world."

The thirty-six-year-old author of *The Sun Also Rises* and *A Farewell to Arms* had planned to take his black, thirty-eight-foot fishing boat, *Pilar*, back to Cuba in the spring of 1935. Unfortunately, the latest Cuban revolt had taken a menacing turn in February. The time had come, he concluded, to switch to the Bahama Islands and do battle with the tuna of Bimini. On April 7, he set out from Key West with a party that included his friend and fellow novelist John Dos Passos and his wife, Katy, artist Mike Strater, backed up by a couple of experienced Conch crewmen, Bread Pinder and Hamilton "Old

Sack of Ham" Adams. Ahead lay a great fishing adventure in Bahamian waters, some 230 nautical miles northeast of Key West.

The trip, launched with such great expectations, lasted only a few hours, just long enough for Ernest to commit one of the most comical blunders of his accident-prone life. In no hurry, Hemingway trolled for fish in the early hours of the journey. Unfortunately for him, he hooked a shark. The author, following his usual procedure, prepared to finish the mighty predator off with a shot from his trusty Colt Woodsman, a .22 caliber pistol, before finally pulling him aboard.

The shark jerked convulsively just as Ernest fired. His shot missed its target, hitting instead a strip of metal along the boat's cockpit. The bullet broke into small pieces and ricocheted into Hemingway's legs.

"I'll be of unsavory parentage," he later claimed he said. "I'm shot."

The author wrote later he felt very little pain, but after having his wounds cleaned and drenched with iodine, he made his way to a bucket and threw up.

"Put her (*Pilar*) around for Key West," said a bloody Hemingway. "Let's see how soon we can make it to the Marine Hospital."

At the hospital, the doctor gave him an anti-tetanus shot and removed most of the small bits of lead. Ernest was kept in bed for three days while doctors watched for signs of infection. No infection developed, so a week after the shooting he set out again for Bimini. This time there was no trolling during the two-hundred-mile cruise. Hemingway turned the shooting to his advantage. He wrote a lighthearted story about it for *Esquire*. It was titled: "On Being Shot Again."

To the Lucayan Indians, the original settlers on the Bahama Islands, Bimini was known as "a healing place" where a sulfur spring gave rise to legends about the Fountain of Youth that so intrigued Ponce de León. To Hemingway it soon became a world of unspoiled beauty—clear, blue waters; a superb beach; adequate docks; one hotel, the Compleat Angler; and just one street, the King's Highway. And in 1935 there wasn't a single automobile on the islands to leak oil on the King's Highway. In a letter to his friend Sara Murphy, Ernest wrote: "It's in the middle of the Gulf Stream and every breeze is a cool one. The water is so clear you think you will strike bottom when you have twelve fathoms under your keel. There is every kind of fish."

"Every kind of fish," but the one he was particularly intrigued by was the horse mackerel, the giant blue-fin tuna that few anglers could bring in intact. The problem was that for most fishermen, reeling in a tuna took so long that sharks bit huge chunks out of the fish. What was finally brought aboard was only part of a fish, said to have been "apple-cored."

The answer, Hemingway concluded, was to bring in his catch as fast as possible. Reel while the tuna was still quick enough to evade the shark. Don't try to tire the fish out; just keep reeling and never let up. The method called for muscle and endurance, and for Hemingway it worked. That spring, Ernest reeled in the first two big, unmutilated tuna ever taken at Bimini. They weighed 514 and 610 pounds. His style was so acclaimed that a fish caught using his approach was said to have been "Hemingwayed."

Hemingway made a big splash in Bimini, and part of it was "on the rocks." In *The Misadventures of a Fly Fisherman*, son Jack wrote: "Papa drank a lot after coming in from fishing and had several fist fights with other visiting sportsmen."

One early evening in May, Ernest was washing down *Pilar* when a voice came to him out of the darkness: "Say, aren't you the guy who claims he catches all the fish?"

"I catch my share," he said as he turned to see a large man in white shorts. Ernest later told Leicester, "I figured him for a mouthy drunk."

The goading continued, including a reference to Ernest as "a big, fat slob." Finally, a barefoot Hemingway leaped up to the dock and clipped the heckler with several lefts, but the man didn't go down.

"Then I backed off and really got the weight of a pivot swing into the old Sunday punch," said Hemingway. "He landed, and his ass and head hit the planking at the same time."

The "mouthy drunk" lay unconscious on the dock while a crowd of some sixty people looked on. The crew from his aptly named boat, *Storm King*, carried him aboard and rushed him to Miami for medical treatment. That night, the writer worried about how seriously his opponent had been hurt. He was even more worried when he found out that the man was Joseph Knapp, owner and publisher of such major American magazines as *Collier's*, *Woman's Home Companion*, *The American Magazine*, and several other publications.

"That's what I call limiting your magazine markets," said Hemingway. The fight, however, as much as his fishing triumphs, transformed him into a legend on the island. Nattie Saunders and a calypso band wrote a song about the fight. It was called "Big Fat Slob."

> Big Fat Slob in the harbor,
> This the night we have fun.
> Oh, the Big Fat Slob in Bimini,
> This the night we got fun.
> Mr. Knapp called Mr. Ernest Hemingway
> A Big Fat Slob.
> Mr. Ernest Hemingway balled his fist
> And gave him a knob.
> Big Fat Slob in Bimini,
> This the night we have fun.

Later that summer, Florida's two most distinguished novelists met in Bimini. Both shared the same Scribner's editor, the fabled Maxwell Perkins. Marjorie Kinnan Rawlings had arrived in Bimini

Boxer Lewis Butler puts on the gloves with Hemingway on the Bimini docks in 1935.

aboard the yacht of Mrs. Oliver Grinnell, an outstanding angler whose husband had caught the first large broadbill swordfish on rod and reel in the Atlantic. Mrs. Grinnell then followed by becoming the first woman to catch a broadbill in the Atlantic. Rawlings, who lived at Cross Creek in central Florida, later wrote Perkins about her meeting with Hemingway: "I'd heard so many tales in Bimini of his going around knocking people down, that I half-expected him to announce in a loud voice that he never accepted introductions to female novelists. Instead, a most lovable, nervous and sensitive person took my hand in a big gentle paw and remarked that he was a great admirer of my work."

The day before she left Bimini, Rawlings saw another side of Hemingway. Word got around that he had caught a 514-pound tuna. Most of the island's population turned out to watch the giant tuna being hoisted up for weighing at the dock. At day's end, a riotously drunk Hemingway used the fish for a punching bag.

Rawlings' *The Yearling* would win a Pulitzer Prize in 1939, some fourteen years earlier than Hemingway's award for *The Old Man and the Sea*. His short novel told the engrossing story of an old fisherman who is robbed of his greatest catch by "apple-coring" sharks.

Fishing was very much on the mind of Hemingway in the summer of 1935, when he met Michael Lerner, president of Lerner Stores Corporation. He was a man as obsessed with the joys of big game fishing as Ernest. Like Hemingway, he was, however, far more than just an enthusiastic angler. Both men were interested in establishing rules, regulations, and an ethical code for fishing and for certifying world-record catches. They were concerned, too, with scientific studies of fish. Lerner funded seven scientific fishing expeditions for the American Museum of Natural History.

Not surprisingly, Bimini's big game fishermen, including Hemingway and Lerner, got together after a day's fishing and drank and talked—and inevitably lied a bit about catches and near-catches. They talked, too, about the need for a sport fishermen's association. In March 1936, Hemingway, never a man for political correctness, wrote to Mike Lerner about some of his ideas about establishing such a club: "Between you and me I think that any sporting organization dominated by a woman, no matter how fine and noble that woman, is a pain in the ass to belong to and I would like to resign as soon as possible. The women I admire in sport fishing are your wife Mrs. Lerner and my wife Mrs. Hemingway and when we are hooked into a fish we don't want any advice from any of them."

The "fine and noble" woman Hemingway was referring to was Marjorie Rawlings' friend, Mrs. Grinnell, or, as he called her, "the 25-hour swordfish queen." She had the nerve to write him a letter blasting him for not attending an important meeting aimed at creating the association.

On July 12, 1936, a group of fishermen gathered at the home of Tommy Shevlin on nearby Cat Cay. Out of that gathering emerged an informal fishing club, the Bahamas Marlin and Tuna Club, whose

International Game Fish Association
Mike Lerner and Ernest Hemingway beam at the size of a
newly caught blue marlin.

goals were to foster better sportsmanship, to establish a smokehouse to preserve marlin and tuna meat that could not be eaten right away, and to encourage greater scientific study of fish. Ernest Hemingway was named president. Lerner and Shevlin were picked as vice presidents, and Kip Farrington, a prolific fishing writer and the first man to land an eleven-hundred-pound fish, was given the job of secretary. The club's members also appointed Earl Roman, the *Miami Herald*'s fishing editor, club historian, apparently assuming they would accomplish something worth remembering. And they did. The small, informal club was the forerunner of the International Game Fish Association, now headquartered at Dania Beach.

Hemingway's letters to Lerner, signed "Ernesto," reveal interesting insights into the thinking of the author, particularly after the

Spanish Civil War began to thrust aside his pursuit of big game fish. In one, he refers to himself good-naturedly as "a big, fat slob like me."

In another, after his work in Spain forced him to step down as president of the club, he expressed his ideas on sportsmanship: "I wanted to resign because I can't be there to look after things now and still think I should. You ought to be president of it, anyway. You are a sportsman. Tommy (Shevlin) is too but he's too young. This confidential. Never let Farrington be president because he is not really a sportsman, maybe he is, I've nothing against him, but he is competitive in a sport where the competition should be all inside yourself and we don't want bickering. He takes it too seriously too. It's serious while you're doing it but we have to remember it's fishing."

In 1938, when the Spanish Civil War had become his main interest, Hemingway sent Lerner "a couple of books" on big game hunting while Mike was recuperating from an illness. The letter that accompanied it is intriguing in light of Ernesto's trouble with excessive drinking: "It's good for us both to lay off the old liquor too; but by God it's dull work doing it. I'd like to hunt and fish the rest of my life and be just drunk enough to sleep well every night and do the drinking with you and Phil Percival (a famous African safari guide) and young Tommy Shevlin. But instead I've got to write, and boil the liquor out to be able to write my best, and get my sensitivity back to be able to write where have sort of burned it away in war. Hell of a job." Hemingway was moving closer to the start of one of his greatest books, *For Whom the Bell Tolls*, and to the end of his marriage to Pauline.

The friendship between Ernest and Lerner lasted the rest of Hemingway's life. When the author bought property in Bimini, Lerner handled the transaction for him. In addition, he used his knowledge of the stock market to buy stock for Hemingway, then sell it and send the gain directly to the author. One letter mentions a check for $1,117.50, profit from the purchase of a stock on a Friday and its sale on a Monday.

By 1939, Lerner's contacts with international fishing organizations had brought the concept of a worldwide organization to a head. On June 7, the International Game Fish Association was launched in a meeting at the American Museum of Natural History in New York. Mike Lerner funded the organization as he had the museum's expeditions. The IGFA's first president was Dr. William King Gregory, head of the departments of ichthyology and comparative anatomy at the museum. Hemingway became a vice president and held the post till his death in 1961. Another Florida author, Philip Wylie of Miami, was also named a field representative and in 1948 a vice president. After Dr. Gregory retired from the museum staff in 1944, Lerner, who lived in Miami, became president. Since 1967, the IGFA has been headquartered in Broward County, first in Fort Lauderdale, then in Pompano Beach, and now in Dania Beach.

Neither Hemingway nor Mike Lerner holds any records, in part because the organization's code of ethics in its early years prohibited any officer from qualifying for a world record catch. To hold a record, an angler's catch must be properly witnessed, weighed at an official weighing station, and documented. Additionally, the line on which the fish was caught must be tested to see that it does not exceed strength specifications.

"At one time Hemingway apparently held at least one Atlantic sailfish record, not well documented," says Michael Leech, IGFA president. "He's in the same position as Zane Grey (the noted author of Westerns who was also a famous game fisherman). Their catches would have been back in the days before lines were tested, so they're not really official IGFA records."

On January 18, 1999, Hemingway was inducted posthumously into the IGFA's World Hall of Fame, one of twenty-nine sportsmen honored in the association's inaugural ceremony. That summer he was further honored at the IGFA's new headquarters/museum with a Hemingway exhibit. It opened on July 21, the one-hundredth anniversary of his birth in Oak Park, Illinois.

BIMINI TODAY

If Hemingway returned to Bimini today, he would find it little changed. The Compleat Angler, a favorite inn and watering hole, is still there. Now it has an entire room, Room 1, dedicated to him, displaying photographs and excerpts from several of his works. The Compleat Angler, which assumed the name of the great fishing classic written in 1653 by the Englishman Izaak Walton, is marketed as "Hemingway's place in Bimini." Mike Lerner's house, the Anchorage, is still around, only now it's a surf-and-turf, dinner-only restaurant. The restaurant is named, appropriately, the Anchorage.

Bimini is now served by two main thoroughfares, the King's Highway and the Queen's Highway. One other item is new: the old Government Administration Building has been restored and now houses the Bimini Museum.

"Hemingway's spirit is very much alive in Bimini," says Sir Michael Checkley, director of the Bimini Museum. "The museum has a wall dedicated to Hemingway. We also have rare videos of E. H. on Bimini with Mike Lerner and also other friends. . . . [and] the weigh scale from Weech's Bimini Dock, the dock used to bring his catch in for weighing."

❖

CHAPTER XV

❖ ❖ ❖ ❖ ❖ ❖ ❖ ❖ ❖ ❖ ❖

CUBA

IT WAS CLEARLY NOT A CASE OF LOVE AT FIRST SIGHT. Ernest Hemingway first saw Havana on April Fool's Day in 1928. He and a pregnant Pauline had sailed from La Rochelle, France, en route to Key West aboard the English steamship *Orita*. Approached from the sea, Havana offers an enchanting vista, the sixteenth-century fortress El Morro on the left and on the right, La Habana Vieja, Old Havana, the heart of the grandest of the Spanish colonial cities. Unfortunately, the Hemingways arrived on a dark, foggy night.

Before proceeding on to Key West aboard a Peninsular & Occidental steamship, the Hemingways rented a car and toured Havana for two days. "Of these first 48 hours of Hemingway in Havana there was not a trace in his works," observed Gabriel Garcia Marquez, one of the most important of all contemporary Hispanic writers.

For the next four years, Ernest returned in the winter to Key West. There his friend, favorite bootlegger, and speakeasy operator, Joe Russell, regaled him repeatedly with tales of fishing for marlin off Cuba, on the south side of the Gulf Stream, just ninety miles from Key West. "Ernest, those big fish are the most exciting thing to catch there is," Joe told Hemingway one afternoon over drinks at Joe's bar.

In the spring of 1932, Hemingway finally acted on Russell's grandiose claims. From the first encounter with the huge marlin of the Gulf Stream, Hemingway was hooked. Fishing in the freshwater streams of Michigan, the American West, or Europe was never like this. Hemingway's ten days of fishing turned into twenty, then stretched almost to seventy, ended only by sickness. Friends, lovers, a wife, a sister, a brother came and went. Ernest stayed. By the end of May he had caught nineteen marlin. He had also caught bronchial pneumonia. In late June he returned to Key West.

Ernest's first extended trip to Havana left him hooked on more than Gulf Stream fishing. Her name was Jane Mason, a tall, gorgeous strawberry blonde. He had met her a year earlier aboard a trans-Atlantic cruise from France to New York.

At eighteen, Jane had married Grant Mason, a major owner of Pan-American Airways. Mason ran the airline's Caribbean operations from Cuba. The size of the territory kept Grant away from home much of the time. And his travels left the beauteous Jane alone, except for a dozen servants, in their tropical mansion on the banks of the Jaimanitas River, just west of Havana. Enter Ernest Hemingway. And quickly.

Like Hemingway, Jane, who piloted her own boat, was an enthusiastic and skillful angler, hunter, and consumer of strong drink. She introduced Hemingway to such glittering cabarets as Sans Souci and was often seen with him at El Floridita, which became his favorite watering hole. Jane has been described as "sensual, extravagant, outrageous," and "wild." Only a few weeks after Hemingway began seeing her, an entry appeared in the log of *Anita* that read "Ernest loves Jane." It was not in Hemingway's handwriting.

The author returned in June to Key West and to his wife and two sons. His next visit to Cuba came the following April. He had planned then for two months of fishing, but this time other problems intruded. In May 1933, Jane was driving her Chevrolet sedan, complete with flashy, yellow wire wheels, back to Jaimanitas, carrying with her Ernest's two older sons, Jack (Bumby) and Patrick. A bus traveling at high speed appeared suddenly. Jane pulled to the edge of the road to avoid the vehicle. The shoulder of the road gave way and the car tumbled down a forty-foot embankment, turning over three times before landing upside down. The doors of the car were jammed but all three managed to crawl out through a front door window.

No one was hurt seriously, but that night Jane embarked on a heavy drinking spree. Two days later, she either jumped or fell from the balcony of her home. She landed in shrubbery but still suffered a broken back in the fall. She was sent to New York for further medical treatment, which included a body cast and extended consultations with a psychiatrist.

Ernest, meanwhile, was busy planning his first safari to Africa, courtesy of a $25,000 gift from Pauline's wealthy uncle, Gus Pfeiffer. In December 1933, Ernest, Pauline, and their friend Charles Thompson arrived at the New Stanley Hotel in Nairobi, Kenya. When the Hemingways returned to America in the winter of 1934, Ernest bought a sportfishing boat, which he named *Pilar*, his secret name for Pauline. It was also a name they had hoped to give to a daughter they now knew they could never have.

In July Hemingway gave *Pilar* her maiden voyage across the Gulf Stream. His crew included two scientists from the Academy of Natural Sciences in Philadelphia, Charles M. B. Cadwalader, director, and Dr. Henry Fowler, chief ichthyologist. Hemingway was becoming a serious student of the marine sciences.

But he was not about to let science move Jane Mason out of the picture. Later that summer, Jane, recovered from her injuries, joined him on a side trip to the storied Archipelago de Camaguey, which stretches for more than four hundred miles along the northeastern coast of the island. Back in Havana with Pauline and the boys, Hemingway resumed his quest for the mighty marlin. He worked hard, too, on his African book. In late October, he returned to Key West, and by the end of November, he had completed the first draft of a book he was calling *The Highlands of Africa.*

On his many trips to Cuba, Hemingway had witnessed a relentlessly unstable political scene, always festering, too often erupting in violence. When he first began to visit the island, it was ruled harshly by the dictator Gerardo Machado. Carlos Manuel de Cespeda overthrew Machado, who fled to Miami on a Pan-American flight arranged by Grant Mason. Twenty-four days later, Sergeant Fulgencio Batista led a revolt that toppled the new government, replacing it with another struggling government that, in turn, lasted four months. Batista took over again and ran Cuba as a dictator for most of Hemingway's years on the island.

In 1935, Hemingway skipped Cuba and visited instead the giant tuna that lived in the waters off Bimini. The following year, civil war erupted in Hemingway's beloved Spain. For the next four years, the writer was so absorbed with the pain and anguish of events in Spain that Key West and Cuba both moved to the back burner.

Then near the end of December 1936, an event occurred that had a profound impact on his commitment to Cuba. In Key West, Martha Gellhorn arrived at Sloppy Joe's bar. Her mission: to meet Hemingway. Gellhorn was a respected newspaper correspondent and novelist in her own right. And clearly an accomplished pick-up artist.

The arrival of Gellhorn on the scene ended what remained of Hemingway's shaky marriage to Pauline. Hemingway and Gellhorn covered the Spanish Civil War together and lived together both in Spain and in Havana. Her preference for a ritzier hotel than the workhorse Ambos Mundos led to a move for the two of them to the Sevilla Biltmore on the fashionable Prado, a dual-laned modern boulevard just west of Old Havana. Hemingway, however, still collected his mail from his original hotel, even from people as close to him as Pauline and Max Perkins. The only way to be left alone, he later explained, was "to tell everybody you live in one hotel and live in another. When they locate you, move to the country."

While living in the Sevilla Biltmore, Ernest began writing the Spanish Civil War novel that would restore him to the loftiest of literary heights. Here he began *For Whom the Bell Tolls.* Martha was not all that happy with the Sevilla and began searching for a house to rent. In April 1939, she found a large farmhouse with six airy, sunlit rooms. Located in the village of San Francisco de Paula, on the outskirts of Havana, it was part of a twenty-one-acre, overgrown estate, somewhat rundown but nicely located on a low hill with its own swimming pool. The rental fee was $100 a month. At her own expense, Martha hired carpenters, painters, two gardeners, and a cook to make La Finca Vigia livable.

On November 4, 1940, Ernest's divorce from Pauline was declared final. Seventeen days later, Ernest and Martha were mar-

John F. Kennedy Library
La Finca Vigia in San Francisco de Paula was the home of Hemingway for most of the last two decades of his life.

John F. Kennedy Library
Hemingway's vast library at the Finca included
nine thousand volumes.

ried by a justice of the peace in Cheyenne, Wyoming. At the end of
December, Ernest bought La Finca for 18,500 pesos, roughly the
same as 18,500 American dollars. It would remain his home for most
of the rest of his life. In his biography of Hemingway, Jeffrey Myers
wrote that Ernest "was thoroughly familiar with the island when he
moved there in 1939. In Havana, his home for the next twenty years,
he found a place that was the exact opposite of Oak Park: Latin,
Catholic, tropical, leisurely, unstable, sinful and corrupt."

The old farmhouse was a comfortable fit for Ernest, pleasant to
live in and remote enough to give him the privacy he needed for his
work. He quickly added the Hemingway touch. Soon, the walls dis-
played trophies from his safari to Africa. Lion- and leopard-skin

John F. Kennedy Library
Hemingway pursued his writing career with the
aid of his friendly cats.

rugs adorned the floors of the library. Bookcases, home to some nine thousand books, appeared in nearly every room.

Instead of an office or a studio, Hemingway preferred to work in his bedroom. He wrote slowly in longhand unless he was writing his incomparable dialogue. The Hemingway dialogue, which flows so swiftly in his stories, moved swiftly, too, in his mind. To keep up with the rhythm of its flow, he stood as he typed dialogue on his Royal portable, which was perched atop a bookcase. He found it more comfortable to type standing. His knee wounds from World War I were now stiffening up again.

At La Finca, Hemingway completed *For Whom the Bell Tolls*, delivering the manuscript to Max Perkins in New York in late July 1940. The book, dedicated to Martha, was published in October to glowing reviews, the best Ernest had received since *A Farewell to Arms*. Within a month, Paramount Pictures had offered him $100,000 for the movie rights. In one sense, it was a great year for both Hemingways. Martha also published a novel, *A Stricken Field*, dedicated to her husband.

The year ahead would bring the most terrible global war the world had ever known. On December 7, 1941, the Japanese attacked Pearl Harbor. The land where Ernest and Martha were born was suddenly plunged into World War II. Both expatriates would become deeply involved.

Hemingway struggled with a basic problem: What can I do for my country? He was too old for the draft and too controversial for some in authority. Since Communists were active in supporting the Loyalists in the Spanish Civil War, others, like Hemingway, who also backed the Loyalists, were viewed with suspicion by many conservatives, particularly J. Edgar Hoover and the Federal Bureau of Investigation. Furthermore, Hemingway was no longer living in the land of his birth but in a country not allied with the United States.

In the winter of 1942, German submarines began torpedoing oil tankers in the Caribbean Sea and the Gulf of Mexico, sinking sixty-eight ships in three months. In the creative whorls of Hemingway's mind, a two-part plan began to emerge. It could be described as patriotic, quixotic, noble, unworkable, naive, crazy, brave, loyal, hopelessly romantic, or all of the above. He gave it a name that only a devilishly imaginative mind could have concocted: the Crook Factory.

Hemingway conceived two schemes to aid the Allied cause. Since Havana harbored many Spanish residents sympathetic to Hitler, Ernest suspected some were feeding damaging information to German submarines preying on tankers and cargo ships in the Caribbean. Why not organize an intelligence-gathering team of Spaniards loyal to a Spanish government that had been overthrown with the aid of Hitler's Germany?

Spruille Braden, the U.S. ambassador to Cuba, gave Ernest the go-ahead, and in a 1971 book, *Diplomats and Demogogues*, he praised the makeshift intelligence operation. Hemingway, he wrote, "enlisted a bizarre combination of Spaniards: some bartenders; a few wharf rats; some down-at-the-heel *pelota* players and former bullfighters; two Basque priests; assorted exiled counts and dukes; several Loyalists and Francistas. He built up an excellent organization and did an A-One job."

Next, Ernest moved ahead with his second scheme, a far more elaborate project. He proposed to convert *Pilar* into a Q-boat, the official designation for a ship or boat armed to wage war while appearing to be a commercial vessel. He planned to recruit a well-trained crew and arm *Pilar* with bazookas, grenades, short-fuse bombs, and .50 caliber machine guns.

Under the command of Admiral Hemingway, the crew would cruise along the north coast of Cuba, pretending to be scientists gathering specimens for the American Museum of Natural History. If a Nazi sub stopped them, they would wait until the craft had moved within fifty yards of *Pilar*. Ernest would close to within twenty yards. Then the crew would begin shooting. Ideally, the heavy machine guns would mow down the men on deck, setting the stage for specially trained crewmen to lob hand grenades down the sub's conning tower. Then, if possible, they would heave one of the short-fuse bombs into the sub's forward hatch.

All Ernest needed was radio equipment, arms, ammunition, official U.S. approval, a sign for *Pilar*'s prow stating she was an American Museum of Natural History boat, a letter from the Navy camouflaging the mission of the good ship *Pilar*—and a boatload of luck. Once again, Ambassador Braden bypassed a few regulations and turned Hemingway loose against the Nazis.

Hemingway's sportfisherman was outfitted at the shipyard at Casablanca on the east bank of the Havana Harbor. Meanwhile, Ernest assembled quite a crew. It included Winston Guest, a millionaire playboy friend who was also the godson and second cousin of Winston Churchill; a couple of Basque jai-alai players; a Marine master sergeant from the Embassy; a Catalonian bartender; and the skipper, Gregorio Fuentes. Rounding out the crew was the admiral himself, Ernest Hemingway.

Martha was not happy with the Crook Factory. She never knew when Ernest's secret agents might pop up or disappear in the dense vegetation at La Finca. He ran them through occasional drills requiring field-stripping and cleaning of guns and sessions of hand-grenade lobbing. Practice runs with *Pilar* were sometimes followed by drinking bouts at unexpected times of the day or night.

Fortunately for Hemingway, who even took his two youngest sons along on one of his trips along the north coast, the Q-boat never encountered any German submarines. By late fall of 1942, Hemingway had grown tired of the sub patrol. "A playboy who hunted submarines off the Cuban coast as a whim," was the assessment of Captain Mario Ramires Delgado, the only captain to sink a German submarine in Cuban waters.

The Crook Factory finally ran afoul of the Federal Bureau of Investigation. The FBI, which eventually took over American intelligence gathering in Cuba, accused Hemingway of being a Communist, partly because of his pro-Loyalist sentiments and partly because he had unwisely introduced an FBI man to a group in Cuba as a Gestapo member. Unfortunately for Hemingway, the FBI kept a file on him for the rest of his life.

Hemingway returned to La Finca but not to writing. He drank heavily and quarreled with Martha as their marriage disintegrated. By early fall of 1943, Martha had lined up a series of assignments as a *Collier's* magazine war correspondent in Great Britain. Shortly before she was to leave, she encountered Dr. Jose Luis Herrera Sotolongo, Ernest's personal physician and a friend since the days of the civil war in Spain.

"I'm saying good-bye to you, Doctor," she told him. "I'm leaving for Europe and I won't be back to the beast." When Herrera asked Hemingway to explain what Martha meant, Ernest gave him a baffling reply, "She's from St. Louis, Missouri." Soon Hemingway arrived in Great Britain as chief correspondent for *Collier's* for the war in Europe. It was not, however, a friendly move. His new post had the nasty effect of weakening Martha's status at the magazine.

Meanwhile, in the spring of 1944, Ernest met Mary Welsh Monks, who worked in the London bureau of *Time*. In her mid-thirties, she wore her curly, honey-blonde hair cut boyishly short, a style he liked. Mary was twice married and her current marriage, like Hemingway's, was already coming apart. On his second date with her, he blurted out that he wanted to marry her.

A few days later, he rode back from a party through the darkness of a London blackout. The English doctor who was driving plowed into a steel water tank. Hemingway was thrown forward into the windshield and his knees were smashed against the dashboard. Doctors at St. George's Hospital took two and a half hours and fifty-seven stitches to close his head wound. Throbbing headaches caused by the concussion were incessant. Mary visited him at the hospital, as did Martha. His reunion with his wife, however, was an ugly one, which ended when Martha told him they were through. He had walked away from his first two marriages. Martha was the first wife to walk out on him.

In August, a jeep accident brought another concussion, more headaches, and now double vision to the accident-prone writer. But before the month was over, Hemingway, battered by concussions, nonetheless reestablished himself as a hero of mythic proportions. On August 25, 1944, American troops liberated Paris—his Paris, the city where he first came alive as a writer. But it was Ernest Hemingway who liberated the Ritz Hotel. Ernest and a band of correspondents he had gathered around him arrived at the hotel. The manager welcomed them back with a huge round of martinis, then served them a superb meal. When Hemingway liberated the Ritz, the world knew he was back in charge again.

The picture soon became even rosier. Mary told him that she would try living with him. By mid-March, Ernest was back in Cuba, still fighting headaches, slowed speech, and some loss of memory. He was joined by Patrick and Gregory. On May 8, 1945, Mary arrived in Havana. It could not have been a more propitious occasion. That same day Germany surrendered. Then in June, oldest son Jack, who had been a prisoner of war, arrived for recuperation from six months in a POW camp.

Before the month was over, however, Ernest had complicated his life again, the victim of another automobile accident, this one with the author himself at the wheel. Once more he injured his head and also broke four ribs. Mary received severe facial cuts. Still, by the end of December, the war was over and Hemingway had cut back on his drinking. He was also back at work on a novel set in Bimini. And to make it complete, both divorce cases, his and Mary's, were finalized. Time for a wedding.

On March 14, 1946, the two-stage marriage ceremony took place in the office of a Cuban lawyer. Before lunch, bride and groom listened to a complete reading of the Spanish version of the Napoleonic Code as it pertained to the property rights of the couple. After lunch, they spoke their vows, then attended a champagne reception. That afternoon, Ernest became quarrelsome and Mary irritable. On the drive back to La Finca, they argued furiously. Mary went to bed alone, wondering if she should pack up and leave the next day. Happy honeymooning ahead? Actually, the next day Ernest was conciliatory and the dispute was smoothed over. It wouldn't exactly be a happy marriage, but at least it would outlast Hemingway's three and Mary's two previous attempts.

Nineteen-forty-six—the first full year after the end of the most terrible war the world had ever known. Time for a new beginning. At La Finca, the man who had just been acclaimed America's best novelist by *The Saturday Review of Literature* could look back at six wartime years

Cruising past Morro Castle, *Pilar* and Mary Hemingway's little boat, *Tin Kid,* head out to the Gulf Stream.

without any published fiction. He had lapsed deep within a mood he called a "black-ass to end all black-ass" depressions. Somehow, like a champion boxer, Ernest Hemingway picked himself up off the floor and returned to what he did best, writing fiction.

Each day at first light, he brushed aside health and mood problems to plunge into a grand project, encompassing the land, air, and sea war during the decade from 1936–1946. The concept started as a single book, then expanded quickly into a multi-volume project that would occupy him for the rest of his life. It would in time be spun off into three separate books, *Across the River and Into the Trees, The Old Man and the Sea,* and *Islands in the Stream,* which would be published posthumously. By the middle of February, Ernest had completed four hundred pages. He was training hard, too, to work himself back into shape for the huge project that lay ahead of him. He wrote in the morning, then in the afternoon swam laps or went deep-sea fishing. He ate an early supper, then listened to music on his Capehart record player before retiring early to read.

By June, he had written a thousand pages. Then in July, Mary, now thirty-eight, gave him the best possible news: she was pregnant. Ernest, father of three sons, had always wanted a daughter. Long before, a name had been assigned to her: Pilar. She would, of course, have to share the name with a boat.

That summer, Ernest and Mary set out for Sun Valley, Idaho, where all three sons were to meet them. At Casper, Wyoming, Mary awoke alone on August 19 with unbearable stomach pains. Her screams reached Ernest, outside their tourist cabin packing the car. He called an ambulance, which rushed her to the county hospital. The doctor on duty determined she was hemorrhaging from a burst fallopian tube. The pregnancy had developed outside her uterus.

Away on a fishing trip, the surgeon for the little hospital did not return until that evening. Late that night, following transfusions of whole blood and plasma, Mary was being prepped for surgery when, suddenly, her veins collapsed. The doctor told Ernest she would die of shock if he operated. It was hopeless. It was time to say his last farewell to his wife.

Hemingway took charge. He had seen enough battlefield transfusions to know what had to be done. He ordered the intern to insert the needle into one of Mary's veins. Still, the plasma would not flow. Ernest, in his own words, "cleared the line by milking the tube down and raising and tilting" until the plasma flowed freely. Mary revived and Hemingway told the surgeon to operate. With the ruptured fallopian tube removed, Mary was out of danger. She did, however, remain under an oxygen tent for a week.

Ernest had saved her life, and Mary never forgot it. For the next two weeks, whenever Mary awoke from her sleep, she saw at her bedside either a private nurse or Ernest. The couple did not return to Cuba until December. Back on the island, Hemingway confronted a series of bizarre events. In April, Patrick arrived after having an automobile accident in Key West. He apparently had suffered an undiagnosed concussion, which developed into a high fever, violent behavior, and delirium. Again, Ernest, helped by Pauline, emerged as a tender and effective caregiver. He slept outside his son's door.

In June, Hemingway lost one of his closest friends and wisest counselors. His beloved editor, Maxwell Perkins, died in New York of a heart attack. Max had worked with him through good times and bad—mostly good, since their association had brought forth *The Sun Also Rises, A Farewell to Arms,* and *For Whom the Bell Tolls.* The following month, Ernest encountered a buzzing in his ears and serious problems with high blood pressure. Furthermore, the turmoil that had engulfed his life wrecked his fitness routine and his weight soared again.

Ahead lay another problem. Confusing rumors began to surface in August after the Cuban minister of defense announced the capture in Cuba of four pilots and their airplanes belonging "to the group that is preparing the much publicized expedition against Santo Domingo." The brutal dictator of the Dominican Republic, Raphael Trujillo, called on the Cuban government to stop the group, which had been assembled on Cayo Confites in the Romano Archipelago. Hemingway, always a foe of dictators, had given money to this ragtag force, unfortunately in the form of easily traceable personal checks. In October, the expedition became international news when the Trujillo government announced it would be taking the case to the International Justice Tribunal at The Hague in the Netherlands. A news story reported that some of the implicated American and Canadian flyers had made a statement that involved Hemingway:

"These men, according to the Dominican report, were given lodging in the home near Havana, Cuba, of the American novelist, Ernest Hemingway, who on several occasions acted as a spokesman for the revolutionaries. The American aviators implicated in the plot returned recently to Miami, Florida, declaring that although they had been well fed and provided with drink in Hemingway's home, they had not been paid the sums they had been promised for their part in the adventure."

Hemingway's close friend, Dr. Jose Luis Herrera Sotolongo, found it hard to believe that Ernest could have been so naive as to write personal checks for such a venture. He understood at once the imminent danger his old friend now faced. There will be arrests, he told Ernest, urging him to flee the country immediately. If they hurried, they could get him on the afternoon flight to New York. Rene Villareal, chief of La Finca's staff, packed a suitcase while Hemingway gave last-minute advice to Mary and to Pauline, Patrick, and Gregory, who were visiting at the time. A furious Hemingway was driven to the airport by his chauffeur. He reached the plane just in time to climb the boarding ladder to safety.

Meanwhile, back at the farm, Mary was startled by the loud barking of their watchdogs. As she went to the front steps, Cuban soldiers appeared from the shrubbery and a young lieutenant aimed his rifle at her. She pushed the barrel down with her hand and said in Spanish, "Put that thing aside. What kind of joke is this?"

He told her she was under arrest. Thinking fast, she claimed she was a captain in the United States Army and was also pregnant. Rene appeared, talked to the soldier, and read the warrant.

"I'm sorry, my senora," he said, "but this appears to be legal. They have the right to search the house."

"We are searching only for guns and ammunition," said the lieutenant.

"You won't find anything," said Mary.

But they did—rifles; shotguns, including one once owned by the Spanish Duke of Alba; Ernest's favorite Winchester pump gun; U.S. and German army pistols; and thousands of shells and boxes of various-sized ammunition. Mary was allowed to change her clothes before being driven to the nearest jail. Two phone calls brought her release. Guns and ammunition were returned the next day.

John F. Kennedy Library
Hemingway and Gregorio Fuentes, one of the models for Old
Man Santiago, display impressive catches: a wahoo, left, and a
billfish.

A few days later, a story in the *Miami Herald* cleared up part of
the fiasco. The Havana-area headquarters of the group had been
reported as the home of an American writer. But it was not
Hemingway. The writer was J. P. McAvoy, the Cuba editor of *Reader's
Digest*.

To continue work on his ambitious sea book, Hemingway headed back to Idaho, far from the islands in the stream and banana-
republic turmoil. In time, Cuba's interest in the Trujillo plot waned.
In February 1948, Ernest returned and resumed his work at La Finca.
He moved quickly into a productive routine, writing, swimming,

and fishing. In June, he had the pleasure of a ten-day party for Patrick, preparing to enter college after his difficult illness the previous year.

In September, Ernest and Mary boarded a cruise ship bound for Genoa, Italy. On the Italian trip he met eighteen-year-old Adriana Ivancich, who would become the inspiration for the heroine in his next novel. Unfortunately, a continuing pattern of illnesses and injuries plagued the Hemingways. Mary broke her right ankle skiing. Then a severe chest cold sent Ernest to bed for two weeks, followed by an erysipelas infection in one eye, watched closely by Padua hospital doctors, who feared the infection might spread to his brain. Later that same year, the Hemingways went skiing again. Same result. Mary broke her other ankle, and Ernest's eye infection returned.

Back in Cuba, Hemingway pushed hard to finish his book, inspired by Adriana. The novel, set in Trieste, Italy, just after the end of World War II, tells the story of Colonel Richard Cantwell, his infatuation with Renata (Adriana), and his struggles to come to terms with a series of heart attacks that have doomed him. Published by Scribner's in September 1950, *Across the River and Into the Trees*, the author's first book in a decade, should have been a literary event. Instead it was a catastrophe. Reviewers were rough, expressing pity and embarrassment, calling the author "a travesty of himself," and describing it as his "worst novel." Maxwell Geismar declared ". . . it throws a doubtful light on the future." Martha Gellhorn wrote a friend that the story had "a long sound of madness and a terrible smell as of decay. . . . I think he (Hemingway) will end in the nut house."

Mary's reaction was even worse. Although the book was dedicated to her, it paraded before the world her husband's infatuation with a teenage girl. Bad reviews may have increased his abusiveness towards Mary. A month after the book came out, Mary asked Charles Scribner to find her a job in New York because Ernest had become so

146

unbearable. Nothing came of her request.

It was a low time in the life of the old competitor. Critics attacked him again on the twenty-fifth anniversary of the publication of *The Sun Also Rises*. Most concluded he would probably never again write anything significant. What they didn't know was that the moody author was entering his last "up" cycle. And the man who had influenced American writing more than any other twentieth-century writer knew what to do with the final return of his focus and his artistry.

By January 1951, Hemingway was at work again, this time on a simple fable of the sea, the tale of an old fisherman even more down in his luck than the author. His fisherman, Santiago, had gone eighty-four days without taking a fish. He was judged by some to be *salao*, "the worst kind of unlucky." Hemingway had gone eleven years without writing a book worthy of his genius. Also *salao*.

The fictional Santiago lived in the very real fishing village of Cojimar, where Hemingway berthed *Pilar*. It was also the hometown of Gregorio Fuentes, who had faithfully captained his boat for a decade and a half. Was Gregorio the "Old Man" of the story or was the hero Carlos Gutierrez, who had first told Hemingway a different kind of fishing story, one he could never forget? Most fishing stories are about how big a fish was. Carlos's story was about how big the heart of the fisherman was.

Or was the "Old Man" Hemingway himself? A man down in his luck, a man about to rise above aging, humiliation, and defeat to catch something bigger than the biggest fish ever caught—a novel that would move the hearts of readers around the world. On September 1, 1952, *Life* magazine printed the twenty-seven-thousand-word story of the old fisherman. Eager readers gobbled up five million copies. A week later, Scribner's published fifty thousand hardback copies of *The Old Man and the Sea*. Critics who had speculated that the Old Man was through turned into cheerleaders.

The Old Man and the Sea is a masterpiece of storytelling: gripping, fast-moving, absorbing. Hemingway carries Santiago—and the reader—through the capture of a fifteen-hundred-pound marlin from a tiny boat, then into his mighty but futile struggles against the sharks that take away all but the skeleton of the biggest fish any of the fishermen of Cojimar have ever seen. As his strength fails, the Old Man tells himself: "But man is not made for defeat. A man can be destroyed but never defeated." Is this Hemingway talking to himself? Or about himself?

Acclaim was quick in coming. Just two weeks after publication came the Medal of Honor from the Cuban Tourism Institute, and the following spring the Pulitzer Prize for Literature. Then, on October 28, 1954, came the magic words ". . . for his mastery of the art of narrative, most recently demonstrated in *The Old Man and the Sea*, and for the influence that he has exerted on contemporary style." Ernest Hemingway was awarded the Nobel Prize for Literature. He followed Sinclair Lewis, Eugene O'Neill, Pearl Buck, and William Faulkner to become only the fifth American writer to win the award.

Poor health blocked him from traveling to Sweden to accept the prize. In fact, his failing health was fast intruding on every aspect of his life. In between his Pulitzer and Nobel Prizes, Ernest had treated himself to one last trip to Africa, this one not for the macho pursuit of lions and water buffalo but for the more serene pleasures of sightseeing. The change of style almost cost him his life.

At the end of the trip, Ernest and Mary took a flight in a small plane to see Murchison Falls. Attempting to avoid a flock of large birds, the pilot struck an abandoned telegraph wire. The Hemingways and the pilot, though injured, all walked away from the crash. Newspapers around the world reported the death of the great author, but he was still alive and kicking when another small plane arrived the next day to rescue them. They climbed aboard for their flight to Entebbe, the capital of Uganda. The rescue plane was airborne only a few seconds before the starboard engine caught fire. All aboard escaped by kicking out the front window—all, that is, except Ernest, who was too big for the narrow opening. He escaped by butting the passenger door open with his head. He escaped the burning plane with his hair afire but would learn later that he had paid a heavy price. More stories of his death surfaced. As had been the case of one of his idols, Mark Twain, he could claim, "Reports of my death have been greatly exaggerated." Twice.

Nearly two months passed before Ernest reached Venice, where less-primitive doctors determined just how serious his injuries had been. His skull was fractured; two spinal discs were cracked; his right arm and shoulder were dislocated; his liver, right kidney, and spleen were ruptured; his sphincter muscle was paralyzed; and his vision and hearing were impaired. The concussion had been his tenth. Many of the problems from the crashes would plague him for the few years that were left in his life.

By 1955, Hemingway had become the most popular man in Havana. He was recognized on the streets with cries of "Papa" and

John F. Kennedy Library
Ernest and Mary Hemingway enjoy cocktails at El Floridita with actor Spencer Tracy, who played the role of Santiago in the movie *The Old Man and the Sea.*

accosted at his favorite bar, El Floridita, where people flocked to say they had shared a daiquiri with the great man, if only at a distance. Limousine tours brought sightseers to La Finca, ignoring the sign in Spanish that warned uninvited visitors to stay away. Working was difficult for him but he stayed active. At La Finca he worked on a novel that would be published posthumously as *The Garden of Eden*. He also began his memoir of the Paris years, *A Moveable Feast*.

Spurred by the Mafia-driven hotel/casino business, Havana was changing before his eyes. Skyscrapers were rising near the beaches, and four-lane highways were altering the look of the countryside. Booming tourism was bringing in travelers, snapping pictures and crowding restaurants and bars. Other changes were coming too. In the mountains to the east, the names Fidel Castro and Che Guevara were starting to be heard in considerably more than a whisper. As the Castro rebellion spread, the Batista government countered with arrests, imprisonment, and torture. A Batista patrol covering the San Francisco de Paula area killed Machakos, one of Ernest's dogs. The time had come for the Hemingways to leave Cuba. Hemingway had seen revolutions before, and he knew rich Americans were fair game in a poor country where overthrow of a government also overthrew all laws.

Ernest, Mary, and Gregorio took *Pilar* far out into the Great Blue River, where they made a strange sacrifice to the gods of war. Inside the boat's bunks Hemingway had concealed a small arsenal. Given the Trujillo incident more than a decade before, what would Batista's forces think if they found far too much armament for a simple sport-fishing boat to justify? Into the Gulf Stream they dumped heavy rifles, sawed-off shotguns, hand grenades, and canisters and belts of ammunition for automatic rifles.

Ernest made only three more visits to Cuba, two short ones in 1959, a longer one in 1960. On his last trip, he met Castro for the first and only time. Fidel had entered the Hemingway Fishing Tournament at Havana's Barlovento Yacht Club. When the Cuban dictator caught a marlin to win first place, Ernest awarded him the winner's trophy. Photographs taken that day are the only ones showing them together. Today these pictures show up in public places all over Havana, implying a closeness that never existed.

Hemingway's health disintegrated, and his depression became deeper. His once-mighty body was now overloaded with a dizzying number of medications and alcohol. At the Mayo Clinic in Rochester, Minnesota, he was treated for hypertension, an enlarged liver, fluctuating blood pressure, diabetes, and depression. He suffered, too, from paranoia, fearful that the FBI was tracking his every move. Actually, they were. They even knew he had checked in at Mayo under an assumed name.

Twice he had tried to commit suicide. Then, at 7:30 A.M. on July 2, 1961, Ernest Hemingway placed a shotgun in his mouth, pulled the trigger, and killed himself. He died in Ketchum, Idaho, far from his beloved Great Blue River and the islands in the stream.

❖

CHAPTER XVI

❖ ❖ ❖ ❖ ❖ ❖ ❖ ❖ ❖ ❖

HEMINGWAY TRAIL IN CUBA

"HEMINGWAY'S IMPACT ON CUBAN tourism is large," says Danilo Arrate, former director of Museo Ernest Hemingway. "The Museo, the Floridita, the Bodeguita, La Terraza, the Ambos Mundos, the Hemingway Marina all draw heavily on Hemingway." In many of the tourist guidebooks, these sites constitute what is now referred to as the Hemingway Trail. They are somewhat spread out, which rules out a walking tour. Three, however, are downtown in Old Havana, within easy walking distance of each other. Let's start with them.

The Ambos Mundos Hotel on Calle Obispo offers a one-room Hemingway museum. Room 511 is now designated Habitacion de Hemingway and is furnished somewhat as it was in his day. The Hemingway motif is strong elsewhere in the hotel, where he is honored by a plaque on the front of the building as well as by numerous photos on the walls of the lobby. In the 1930s, Hemingway paid $2 a night for a room. Visitors to the museum can see it for $1, unless they are hotel guests, for whom admission is free.

El Floridita, the bar Hemingway visited after a day of writing, lies farther west on Calle Obispo. He was such a fixture there that a particular bar stool was designated as his. No one else sat on it then—or sits on it now. Behind the stool is a bust of Hemingway, and nearby, a photo of him and Castro at their only meeting. It was at El Floridita that a special daiquiri, called the Papa Dobles or the Hemingway Special—at all times delicious—was developed.

La Bodeguita del Medio, located just off Catedral Plaza near Catedral de la Habana, is a lively bar/restaurant that features authentic Cuban food such as pork, black beans, and rice, as well as a popular island drink called the *mojito*. It is probably the *mojito* that fills this lively bodega with so many tourists because this tasty rum drink provides a connection to Hemingway. On a wall behind the bar is a framed written statement that reads: "My Mojito in La Bodeguita, My Daiquiri in Floridita." It is signed by Ernest Hemingway. The joker is this: the sweet, minty *mojito* was not a drink he particularly liked. The endorsement was simply a favor to a friend who needed a boost. No matter; it's worth a stop on the trail.

Cojimar, home port to Hemingway's *Pilar* in the boat's glory days, is a small, picturesque fishing village just six miles east of Havana. It is also the hometown of Santiago, the protagonist in *The Old Man and the Sea*, and of Gregorio Fuentes, Hemingway's pilot and a major model for Santiago. Visitors can visit the waterfront, see the bronze Hemingway bust donated by the port's fishermen, and enjoy good seafood at La Terraza, which had been a hangout for both Ernest and Gregorio, a "very old man of the sea," who died in January 2002 at age 104.

Hemingway Marina, on the west side of Havana, never figured in the author's life in Cuba. Built long after Hemingway's death, it provides a modern marina for deep-sea fishermen, sailors, and divers, and for fishing tournaments. Hemingway is honored in the name of its principal hotel, The Old Man and the Sea, and the restaurant Papa's Restaurant/Bar.

Museo de Hemingway, the author's home during most of his years in Cuba, provides the high point of any aficionado's pilgrimage on the Hemingway Trail. La Finca Vigia is located atop a small hill in the suburb of San Francisco de Paula, seven miles south of

Havana. Visitors are not allowed into the house, partly to prevent theft of valuable artifacts and partly to protect the house and its furnishings from heavy tourist traffic. Fortunately for sightseers, the house has large windows. Visitors can walk around the exterior and peer in at each accessible window, usually staffed by knowledgeable guides proficient in English. On the grounds amid lush tropical vegetation, *Pilar* sits under a protective roof. The swimming pool, now drained of water, is the same one Ernest sometimes commanded his guests to treat with reverence. Why? Because actress Ava Gardner swam naked in the pool, as did Ernest and Mary. Hemingway is gone, Mary is gone, Ava is gone, but La Finca still is alive and well. Go to San Francisco de Paula and pay your respects to one of the true titans of American literature.

❖

A HEMINGWAY CHRONOLOGY

July 21,1899 - Ernest Miller Hemingway born in Oak Park, Illinois

July 8, 1918 - EH wounded while serving in Italy as World War I ambulance driver

September 3, 1921 - EH marries Hadley Richardson in Horton Bay, Michigan; marriage lasts not quite six years

1926 - *The Sun Also Rises* published

May 10, 1927 - EH marries Pauline Pfeiffer in Paris

April 1, 1928 - EH arrives in Havana on way to Key West

September 27, 1929 - *A Farewell to Arms* published

April 29, 1931 - Hemingways acquire home on Whitehead Street

1932 - *Death in the Afternoon* published

1933 - *Winner Take Nothing* published

December 20, 1933 - EH begins two-month African safari

May 1934 - *Pilar* arrives in Key West

April 7, 1935 - EH shoots himself in both legs

1935 - *Green Hills of Africa* published

1936 - Two major stories published: "The Snows of Kilimanjaro" in *Esquire* and "The Short Happy Life of Francis Macomber" in *Cosmopolitan*

July 1936 - Spanish Civil War begins

December 1936 - Martha Gellhorn meets EH in Sloppy Joe's on Greene Street, Key West

October 15, 1937 - EH's Key West novel, *To Have and Have Not*, published

1938 - *The Fifth Column and the First Forty-Nine Stories* published

December 26, 1939 - EH moves from Key West to La Finca Vigia in San Francisco de Paula, Cuba

1940 - *For Whom the Bell Tolls* published

November 21, 1940 - EH marries Martha Gellhorn in Cheyenne, Wyoming, seventeen days after divorce from Pauline is final

December 7, 1941 - Japan bombs Pearl Harbor; U.S. enters World War II

Spring 1942 - EH starts private wartime intelligence network and a

German submarine–chasing operation called the Crook Factory

May 1944 - EH flies to London to begin coverage of the war for *Collier's* magazine; meets Mary Welsh Monks

August 1944 - EH and his "irregulars" liberate the Ritz Hotel in Paris

December 21, 1945 - Martha divorces EH

March 14, 1946 - EH weds Mary Monks in Havana

August 1946 - After Mary's fallopian tube bursts from ectopic pregnancy, EH saves her life on Wyoming operating table after surgeon gives up on her

August 1947 - EH becomes involved in Dominican Republic coup; forced to flee Cuba to avoid arrest

September 7, 1950 - *Across the River and Into the Trees* published; reviews extremely negative

October 1, 1951 - Pauline Hemingway dies suddenly in Los Angeles of tumor in the adrenal medulla

September 1952 - *The Old Man and the Sea* published in *Life* magazine and in book form by Scribner's; reaction of critics and readers overwhelmingly favorable

May 1953 - *Old Man* wins Pulitzer Prize

January 23–24, 1954 - EH and Mary suffer serious injuries in plane crashes on two successive days in Africa; EH reported dead in international press

October 1954 - Hemingway awarded Nobel Prize for literature

December 31, 1958 - Fidel Castro overthrows Batista government in Cuba

April 1959 - EH buys home in Ketchum, Idaho

July 25, 1960 - EH and Mary leave Havana for last time

October–November 1960 - EH's mental and physical health deteriorates sharply

July 2, 1961 - Ernest Hemingway, on third suicide attempt, kills himself in Ketchum, Idaho

BIBLIOGRAPHY

Baker, Carlos. *Ernest Hemingway: A Life Story.* New York: Charles
   Scribner's Sons, 1969.

Baker, Carlos, ed. *Ernest Hemingway: Selected Letters, 1917–1961.* New York:
   Scribner's, 1981.

Brian, Denis. *The True Gen: An Intimate Portrait of Hemingway by Those Who
   Knew Him.* New York: Dell Publishing, 1988.

Bruccoli, Matthew J., ed. *Conversations with Ernest Hemingway.* Jackson,
   MS: University Press of Mississippi, 1986.

———, ed. *The Only Thing That Counts: The Ernest Hemingway–Maxwell
   Perkins Conversation.* New York: Scribner, 1996.

Davis, Elmer. "New World Symphony." *Harpers Magazine* (May 1935).

Day, Jane. "Bimini, Bahamas: Hemingway's Island in the Stream." *South
   Florida History Magazine* (fall 1989).

de Groot, John. "A Farewell to Papa." *Sunshine Magazine* (January 6, 1984).

———. *Papa.* Boise, ID: Hemingway Western Studies Center, 1989.

Dos Passos, John. *The Best Times.* New York: New American Library, 1966.

———. "Old Hem Was a Sport." *Sports Illustrated.* (June 29, 1964).

Farrington, S. Kip, Jr. *Atlantic Game Fishing.* New York: Kennedy, 1937.

Fuentes, Norberto. *Hemingway in Cuba.* Secaucus, NJ: Lyle Stuart, 1984.

A Guide to Key West. New York: Hastings House, 1941.

Heidelberg, Paul. "Boxer Hemingway Laced His Punches With Tips to His
   Sparring Partners." *Sports Illustrated.* (December 23–30, 1985).

Hemingway, Gregory H. *Papa: A Personal Memoir.* Boston: Houghton
   Mifflin, 1976.

Hemingway, Jack. *Misadventures of a Fly Fisherman.* Dallas: Taylor
   Publishing, 1986.

Hemingway, Leicester. *My Brother, Ernest Hemingway.* Sarasota, FL:
   Pineapple Press, 1996.

Hemingway, Lorian. "Leicester: The Other Hemingway." *Clockwatch
   Review,* 3, vol. III, no. 2 (1986).

Hemingway, Mary Welsh. *How It Was.* New York: Knopf, 1976.

Hotchner, A. E. *Papa Hemingway*. New York: Random House, 1966.

Houk, Walter. "On the Gulf Stream Aboard Hemingway's *Pilar*." *North Dakota Quarterly*, vol. 65, no. 3 (1998).

Kaufelt, Lynn Mitsuko. *Key West Writers and Their Houses*. Sarasota, FL: Pineapple Press/Omnigraphics, 1986.

Kert, Bernice. *The Hemingway Women*. New York: Norton, 1983.

Langley, Joan, and Wright Langley. *Key West: Images of the Past*. Key West: C. C. Belland and E. O. Swift, 1982.

Langley, Wright, and Stan Windhorn. *Yesterday's Key West*. Miami: Seemann Publishing, 1973.

Lynn, Kenneth S. *Hemingway*. New York: Ballantine, 1987.

McLendon, James. *Papa: Hemingway in Key West*. Key West: Langley Press, 1990.

Mellow, James R. *Hemingway: A Life Without Consequences*. New York: Houghton Mifflin, 1992.

Meyers, Jeffrey. *Hemingway: A Biography*. New York: Harper & Row, 1985.

Miller, Linda Patterson. "The Matrix of Hemingway's *Pilar* Log, 1934–1935." *North Dakota Quarterly*, vol. 64, no. 3. (1997).

Nakjavani, Erik. "Hemingway's 'The Great Blue River': The Gulf Stream as the Great Mother." *North Dakota Quarterly*, vol. 66, no. 2 (1999).

Plath, James, and Frank Simons, eds. *Remembering Ernest Hemingway*. Key West: The Ketch & Yawl Press, 1999.

Putney, Michael. "Key West: Papa Still Remembered." *The National Observer* (August 23, 1975).

Reiger, George. *Profiles in Salt Water Angling*. Englewood Cliffs, NJ: Prentice-Hall, 1973.

Reynolds, Michael. *Hemingway: An Annotated Chronology*. Detroit: Omnigraphics, 1991.

———. *Hemingway: The 1930s*. New York: Norton, 1997.

———. *Hemingway: The Final Years*. New York: Norton, 1999.

Rollyson, Carl. *Nothing Ever Happens to the Brave: The Story of Martha Gellhorn*. New York: St. Martin's, 1990.

Rovere, Richard R. "End of the Line." *The New Yorker* (December 15, 1951).

BIBLIOGRAPHY

Samuelson, Arnold. *With Hemingway: A Year in Key West and Cuba*. New York: Random House, 1984.

Saunders, Ashley B. *History of the Bahamas: Bimini, a Case Study*. Bimini: New World Press, 1989.

Watson, William Braasch. "Hemingway in Bimini." *North Dakota Quarterly*, vol. 63, no. 3 (1996).

Wells, Sharon. *Sloppy Joe's Bar: The First Fifty Years*. Key West: Key West Saloon, 1983.

White, William, ed. *By-Line: Ernest Hemingway*. New York: Scribner's, 1967.

INDEX

If you enjoyed reading this book, here are some other books from Pineapple Press on related topics. For a complete catalog, write to Pineapple Press, P.O. Box 3889, Sarasota, FL 34230 or call 1-800-PINEAPL (746-3275). Or visit our website at www.pineapplepress.com.

The Florida Chronicles by Stuart B. McIver. A series offering true-life sagas of the notable and notorious characters throughout history who have given Florida its distinctive flavor. **Volume 1**: *Dreamers, Schemers and Scalawags* ISBN 1-56164-155-3 (pb); **Volume 2**: *Murder in the Tropics* ISBN 1-56164-079-4 (hb); **Volume 3**: *Touched by the Sun* ISBN 1-56164-206-1 (hb)

The Florida Keys by John Viele. The trials and successes of the Keys pioneers are brought to life in this series, which recounts tales of early pioneer life and life at sea. **Volume 1**: *A History of the Pioneers* ISBN 1-56164-101-4 (hb); **Volume 2**: *True Stories of the Perilous Straits* ISBN 1-56164-179-0 (hb); **Volume 3**: *The Wreckers* ISBN 1-56164-219-3 (hb)

Florida Portrait by Jerrell Shofner. Packed with hundreds of photos, this word-and-picture album traces the history of Florida from the Paleo-Indians to the rampant growth of the late twentieth century. ISBN 1-56164-121-9 (pb)

Florida's Past Volumes 1, 2, and 3 by Gene Burnett. Collected essays from Burnett's "Florida's Past" columns in *Florida Trend* magazine, plus some original writings not found elsewhere. Burnett's easygoing style and his sometimes surprising choice of topics make history good reading. **Volume 1** ISBN 1-56164-115-4 (pb); **Volume 2** ISBN 1-56164-139-1 (pb); **Volume 3** ISBN 1-56164-117-0 (pb)

Historic Homes of Florida by Laura Stewart and Susanne Hupp. Seventy-four notable dwellings throughout the state—all open to the public—tell the human side of history. Each is illustrated by H. Patrick Reed or Nan E. Wilson. ISBN 1-56164-085-9 (pb)

Houses of St. Augustine by David Nolan. A history of the city told through its buildings, from the earliest coquina structures, through Colonial and Victorian times, to the modern era. Color photographs and original water-colors. ISBN 1-56164-069-7 (hb); 1-56164-075-1 (pb)

Key Biscayne by Joan Gill Blank. This engaging history of the southernmost barrier island in the U.S. tells the stories of its owners and would-be owners. ISBN 1-56164-096-4 (hb); 1-56164-103-0 (pb)

Key West Gardens and Their Stories by Janis Frawley-Holler. Sneak a peek into the lush, tropical gardens of old Key West. Enjoy beautiful views of the islanders' sanctuaries as well as fascinating stories and histories of the grounds where gardens now grow. ISBN 1-56164-204-5 (pb)

My Brother, Ernest Hemingway by Leicester Hemingway. First published in 1962, this updated edition includes a selection of letters from Ernest to his family never before published. If you want to know who Ernest Hemingway really was, read this book. ISBN 1-56164-098-0 (hb)

Over Key West and the Florida Keys by Charles Feil. A gorgeous album featuring aerial photographs of islands large and small, glistening waters, and serene communities. Captions provide bits of Keys history. ISBN 1-56164-240-1 (hb)

Southeast Florida Pioneers by William McGoun. Meet the pioneers of the Palm Beach area, the Treasure Coast, and Lake Okeechobee in this collection of well-told, fact-filled stories from the 1690s to the 1990s. ISBN 1-56164-157-X (hb)